THE POCKET IDIOT'S GUIDE TO

Italian

by Gabrielle Euvino

alpha
books

©1999 Gabrielle Euvino

International Standard Book Number: 0-02-863147-1
Library of Congress Catalog Card Number: 97-80973

05   04   03   8   7   6   5   4

Interpretation of the printing code: the rightmost number of the first series of numbers is the year of the book's printing; the rightmost number of the second series of numbers is the number of the book's printing. For example, a printing code of 99-1 shows that the first printing occurred in 1999.

Printed in the United States of America

Publisher: Kathy Nebenhaus
Editorial Director: Gary M. Krebs
Managing Editor: Bob Shuman
Marketing Brand Manager: Felice Primeau
Development Editors: Phil Kitchel, Jennifer Perillo, Amy Zavatto
Assistant Editor: Georgette Blau
Production Editor: Jenaffer Brandt
Cover Designer: Mike Freeland
Photo Editor: Richard H. Fox
Illustrator: Jody P. Schaeffer
Designer: Glenn Larsen
Indexer: Angie Bess
Production Team: Marie Kristine P. Leonardo, Angel Perez, Gina Rexrode

Contents

Introduction

Will this book make you fluent in Italian? Unless you're a member of MENSA, probably not. But don't dismay—this is the perfect introduction to *la bella lingua* of Italian and after reading through this book, you will be one step closer to realizing your dream of speaking Italian.

About This Book

This book gives you lists of helpful vocabulary and phrases and tells you exactly what you need to say (and how to say it) in myriad situations; at the train station, at your hotel, in a restaurant, at the pharmacy, etc. It also summarizes grammar, vocabulary, and verbs in the most concise manner possible, explaining how it all works and what you can do to start speaking the language immediately. Refer to Appendix B, "Idiot Speak at a Glance," for a handy reference of essential phrases.

Extras to Help You Along

Besides the idiomatic expressions, helpful phrases, lists of vocabulary words, and down-to-earth grammar, this book has useful information provided in sidebars throughout the text. These elements are distinguished by the following icons:

Fast Forward

Here you'll find suggestions and helpful tips on how to utilize your Italian in everyday situations.

Attenzione!

Careful! These boxes tell you when you should pay attention to a particular challenge or situation. (Linguistically, that is!)

Something Extra

These "perks" give you a better understanding of the Italian culture and language.

Acknowledgements

This pocket edition is dedicated to my two feline friends, Eclipse and Bug. It was not intentional that they both be named after cars. It would be quite lonely writing all day without their company and they make me smile and when I smile, I'm happier, and when I'm happier, I'm nicer, and when I'm nice, the world is nice back, and there you have it. Thanks guys, I love you. Corny, but true.

There are a few humans I'd like to thank too. Of course you, Robert, who happens to be both a friend, and a great brother. For all to know, I am so proud to be related to you.

A big *grazie* to Stefano Spadoni and Anna Maria Pellegrino, my technical editors.

And the same goes for those special friends. I so appreciate the love and support you have shown me during the writing of this *libro*: Jessica Mezyk, Ellen McFaul, Hege Steen, Mike Donnally, Beth Walden, Steve Ellison, Kilian Ganly, Maggie, Marc and Tony Salamone and, finally, Colin Chesleigh—whose patience, kindness and generosity humble me to be my best.

Chapter 1

Immerse Yourself

In This Chapter

➤ Tricks of the trade

➤ History of Italian language

➤ Cognates

➤ Pronunciation guide

The Pocket Idiot's Guide to Italian is a book written for any-one on the go. Until now, learning Italian has been a dream, something you wished you could do but never dared. You've finally decided you are going to learn the language and there's no time to waste. *Immersione* is key here, and you'll need to create opportunities for yourself if jumping on a plane and buying a villa in Toscana isn't an option at this particular *momento*. Naturally, you have been immersing yourself in the food of Italy and can boil a mean pot of water. There are a few additional things you can to do enhance your language study:

Invest in a good bilingual dictionary, preferably one printed in Italy. (Garzanti or Zanichelli are both excellent.)

Call your local university and investigate whether it has an Italian department. Find out if it has a mailing list for events and make a point of meeting other "Italophiles."

Rent an Italian movie every week. Listen to the actors and read the words while you try to make out the different words within each sentence. Isolate words that are repeated.

Pick up a box of flash cards at any bookstore, or make your own using that unused box of business cards from your old job.

Listen to the Italian news station, RAI while you clean your house.

A Short Story

The *storia* (history) of the Italian language spans centuries and begins with classical Latin, the literary language of ancient *Roma*, hence the term Romance languages (of which French, Spanish, Portuguese, and Rumanian are also derived). These languages were once called Vulgar Latin because they were offshoots, or dialects, of Latin and spoken by the common people. Italian is the Romance language closest to Latin.

Languages are like seeds that are pulled from one area into another along an air current, germinating wherever there is ripe soil. Latin made its way into English during the seventh century when England converted to Christianity, and later during a revival in classical scholarship stemming from the Renaissance (*rinascimento*, literally meaning "re-birth"). During the sixteenth and seventeenth centuries, hundreds of Latin words were incorporated into English, resulting in much of today's legal and medical terminology. As a result, many words in modern English have their origins in Latin, a hop from Italian.

Dialect

A dialect is a variation of a language, usually particular to a region and often quite different from the standard vernacular spoken. Due to its shape and long history of outside influences, Italy has hundreds of different dialects, many of which are still used today. Some dialects greatly resemble Italian, with particular colloquialisms and idiomatic expressions only understood by those familiar with the dialect. Other dialects are practically different languages. For example, up north in Lombardia, one hears a specifically German accent and a softening of the Rs, a result of the district having once been ruled by Austria. In the Piedmont region, one can hear the French influence. Down south near Napoli, Spanish and French can be heard, whereas in Calabria, certain speech parts are quite clearly Greek (*kalimera* means literally "Good day" in modern Greek) or Albanian in nature. The islands of Sardegna and Sicilia also have their own languages.

Many Italian immigrants brought their dialects to the United States, where they were further influenced by factors such as culture, English, and other dialects. This explains, in part, why the Italian spoken by many immigrants often differs greatly from the Italian that is presented in this book and why you may still have difficulty communicating with your grandmother after having mastered the basics. There are many variations or dialects of Italian spoken around the world today, in such places as Switzerland and many parts of South America.

Tuscan Italian

In modern Italy, the standard language taught in schools and spoken on television is Tuscan Italian, primarily because this was the regional dialect used by the great medieval writers Dante, Petrarca, and Boccaccio, who used what was then only a spoken language. Modern Italian is often quite different from the Italian used during the

Middle Ages, but, as when you compare modern English to Old English, there are many similarities. Look at an excerpt from Dante's *Inferno*:

> *Nel mezzo del cammin di nostra vita*
> *mi ritrovai per una selva oscura,*
> *che la diritta via era smarrita.*

Note the translation:

> *In the middle of our life's journey*
> *I found myself in a dark wood,*
> *out of which the straight way was lost.*

The Italian has a wonderful rhyme quality, the word *vita* working with the word *smarrita*, something which is lost in the translation. Not understanding the Italian, you can still get an idea of the musicality of the language. In fact, it's easy to rhyme in Italian because of the endings. The translation, however, still does not do justice to the flow and meaning of the poem. You can get a sense of what is being communicated, but it's not the same as the original. It's like looking at a photograph of a bright, sunny day where you can see the colors but you can't feel the warmth of the sun, experience the expanse of blue sky, or hear the wind.

Cognates: A Bridge Between Languages

What if you were told that you were already halfway to speaking Italian? The list of Italian words you already know is longer than you can imagine. Some are virtually the same, whereas most are easily identified by their similarity to English. Any words that are similar to and look the same as other words in a foreign language are called *cognates*, or in Italian, *parole simili* (literally, "similar words").

Cognates show that languages are all connected. What is *importante* to remember is that the context of a given subject reveals a great deal of itself to the attentive listener. An isolated word may or may not evoke understanding, but when you see that word in relationship (or *in relazione*) to the *situazione*, you can understand a great deal.

If It Looks Like a Duck...

The Italian language has only a few perfect cognates—such as the words *banana, idea, opera, panorama, pizza, via,* and *zebra*—where the English and the Italian are exactly the same, but it does possess many near cognates. Although not exactly the same, the meanings of near cognates are unmistakable. The endings and pronunciation may be slightly different, but the words are essentially the same. Look at Table 1.1 to get an idea of how many *parole simili* exist between Italian and English.

Table 1.1   Cognates

Aggettivi (Adjectives)	Nomi Maschili (Masculine Nouns)	Nomi Feminili (Feminine Nouns)
americano	l'aeroplano	l'agenzia
blu	l'aeroporto	l'arte
canadese	l'anniversario	la banca
cattolico	l'appartamento	la carota
curioso	l'attore	la città
delizioso	l'autobus	la classe
desideroso	il caffè	la condizione
differente	il centro	la conversazione
difficile	il cinema	la cultura
elegante	il colore	la curiosità
energico	il continente	la depressione
famoso	il cotone	la dieta
frequente	il dizionario	la differenza

continues

Table 1.1   Continued

Aggettivi (Adjectives)	Nomi Maschili (Masculine Nouns)	Nomi Feminili (Feminine Nouns)
grande	il dottore	la discussione
importante	il gruppo	l'emozione
impossibile	l'idiota	l'esperienza
incredibile	il limone	l'espressione
intelligente	il meccanico	la farmacia
interessante	il motore	la festa
lungo	il museo	la fontana
magnifico	il naso	la forma
moderno	l'odore	la fortuna
naturale	l'ospedale	l'identità
necessario	il palazzo	l'inflazione
numeroso	il paradiso	la lettera
popolare	il parco	la lista
possibile	il presidente	la medicina
povero	il programma	la musica
rapido	il rispetto	la persona
ricco	il ristorante	la possibilità
serio	il salario	la probabilità
sicuro	il servizio	la professione
sincero	lo spirito	la regione
splendido	lo studente	la religione
stupido	il supermercato	la rosa
terribile	il teatro	la stazione
tropicale	il telefono	la temperatura
violento	il terrazzo	la turista
virtuoso	il treno	la violenza

Something Extra

The following endings generally translate from English to Italian. (Note that there are always exceptions to every rule.)

The ending **-ty** in English corresponds to *-tà* in Italian.

The ending **-tion** in English corresponds to *-zione* in Italian.

The ending **-ble** in English corresponds to *-ibile* in Italian.

The ending **-ent** in English corresponds to *-ente* in Italian.

The ending **-ence** in English corresponds to *-enza* in Italian.

The ending **-ism** in English corresponds to *-ismo* in Italian.

The ending **-ous** in English corresponds to *-oso* in Italian.

Many English words have been incorporated into the Italian language, including words such as *bar, computer, film, sport,* and *zoo.*

Verb Cognates

There are many Italian verb cognates as well. There are three kinds of verb endings, *-are, -ere,* and *-ire,* or verb families. These verbs are considered regular because all verbs in the same family follow the same rules. Then, of course, there are a few misbehaving verbs, which are considered *irregular.* The only way to remember how an irregular verb works is to memorize it. Take a look at Table 1.2 to see if you can determine the meanings of the verb cognates listed.

Attenzione!

A *false cognate* is a word in Italian that sounds like an English word but means something different. Fortunately, in Italian there aren't many false cognates, or *falsi amici*.

assumere	to hire
camera	room
caro	expensive
coincidenza	connection
come	how
con	with
fabbrica	factory
fattoria	farm
firma	signature
libreria	bookstore
parente	relative
pretendere	to demand

Table 1.2 Verb Cognates

-are verbs	-ere verbs	-ire verbs
anticipare	assistere	attribuire
arrivare	consistere	convertire
celebrare	decidere	diminuire

-are verbs	-ere verbs	-ire verbs
conversare	descrivere	finire
eliminare	discutere	istruire
entrare	dividere	obbedire
invitare	intendere	offrire
passare	offendere	preferire
preparare	ricevere	prevenire
studiare	rispondere	
telefonare	scrivere	
usare	vendere	

Something Extra

An infinitive of a verb is a verb that has not been conjugated, such as, "to be." A conjugated verb is simply a form of the verb that agrees with the subject, such as, "I am," or "you are." When you look up a verb in a dictionary, it is important to look it up under its infinitive form.

Pronunciation

Italian is quite easy to pronounce because it is phonetic, meaning that what you see is pretty much what you say. In this respect, it's a lot easier than English with its silent letters and illogical letter combinations. Why is the word telephone written with a "ph" instead of an "f," and what is that silly "e" doing at the end of it anyway? A child just learning to string letters together will tell you it should be spelled "telefon" and the tot would be right. In Italian, the word is *telefono* and it is pronounced just like it is written. You'll find that the spelling of Italian is easy and, once you get the hang of it, the pronunciation is just as sensible.

Don't Get Stressed Out

In Italian, knowing where to put the stress can sometimes be tricky (or stressful!). As a rule, most words are stressed on the next-to-last syllable, such as *giorno* (**joR**-noh), *signorina* (see-nyoh-**Ree**-nah), and *minestrone* (mee-neh-**stRoh**-neh). Many words are stressed on the third-to-last syllable, such as *automobile* (ow-toh-**moh**-bee-leh) and *dialogo* (dee-**ah**-loh-goh). Stress should be placed on the last syllable when you see an accent mark at the end of a word, such as *città* (chee-**tah**), *così* (koh-**zee**), and *virtù* (veeR-**too**).

Attenzione!

Always remember to enunciate vowels clearly and not to slur your words. Say what you see.

Right now it seems like a lot of rules with just as many exceptions, but your brain will naturally pick up where to put the stress without a lot of headaches. This is the "fuzzy" period of language learning, much like having a box filled with puzzle pieces that haven't been fit together yet. At first, it's all just a jumble of sounds and letters and words, but slowly, almost imperceptibly, your confusion is replaced with understanding. Language learning is an intuitive process. Knowing this might help you overcome your initial frustration and confusion.

Something Extra

For the purposes of clarity, the pronunciation used in this text is designed to be read phonetically.

Rs are trilled and capitalized to remind you of their importance.

Double *RRs* should be held and emphasized when trilled.

Double consonants should always be emphasized—however, not as separate sounds. They should be joined and slide into one another, as in the word *pizza* (*pee-tsah*).

Your ABCs

Like English, the Italian language uses the Latin alphabet. Unlike English, however, the Italian alphabet contains only 21 letters. If you've ever studied another Romance language, you'll have no problem with the pronunciation because the vowels are pronounced similarly. For first-time language learners, follow the rules as outlined in this chapter. Try not to overstress letters or syllables when you pronounce words; you'll end up appearing like someone trying to sound Italian instead of sounding like an Italian speaker. Speak with care; no lazy mouths please!

There are a few sounds in Italian that are not found in English, the most obvious being the rolled *R*. Some people can roll their *Rs* forever, but if you're not one of them, place the tip of your tongue so that it's touching the roof of your mouth just behind your front teeth. Now curl the tip of your tongue and exhale. You should get the beginning trill of a rolled *R*. If you're still not successful, do this while you're in the shower with the water running through your mouth. If that doesn't work, imagine you're a purring kitten happily kneading a pillow or an opera singer in Carnegie Hall. Whatever you do, keep trying. Even without a perfect *R*, however, you'll still be able to get your message across.

Vowels (Vocali)

The word for vowel in Italian (*vocale*) sounds just like the English word for vocal. Italian vowels are always pronounced clearly and are never slurred. If you can master the vowels, you're already halfway to the point of sounding Italian. Table 1.3 shows how the vowels are pronounced. Read aloud to practice.

Table 1.3 Pronouncing Vowels Properly

Vowel	Sound	Example	Pronunciation
a	ah	*artista*	ahR-tee-stah
e	eh	*elefante*	eh-leh-fahn-teh
i	ee	*isola*	ee-zoh-lah
o	oh	*opera*	oh-peh-Rah
u	oo	*uno*	oo-noh

A

Say *ah* as in "father":

madre	fila	canto	casa	strada	mela
mah-dReh	*fee-lah*	*kahn-toh*	*kah-zah*	*stRah-dah*	*meh-lah*
(mother)	(thread)	(song)	(home)	(street)	(apple)

E

Say *eh* as in "make" or "let":

padre	sera	festa	bene	età	pensione
pah-dReh	*seh-Rah*	*feh-stah*	*beh-neh*	*eh-tah*	*pen-see-oh-neh*
(father)	(evening)	(party)	(well)	(age)	(motel)

I

Say *ee* as in "feet":

idiota	piccolo	pulire	in	idea	turista
ee-dee-oh-tah	*pee-koh-loh*	*poo-lee-Reh*	*een*	*ee-deh-ah*	*too-Ree-stah*
(idiot)	(small)	(to clean)	(in)	(idea)	(tourist)

O

Say *oh* as in "note" or "for":

donna	bello	cosa	albero	gatto	uomo
doh-nah	*beh-loh*	*koh-zah*	*ahl-beh-Roh*	*gah-toh*	*woh-moh*
(woman)	(beautiful)	(thing)	(tree)	(cat)	(man)

U

Say *oo* as in "crude":

luna	una	cubo	lupo	tuo
loo-nah	*oo-nah*	*koo-boh*	*loo-poh*	*too-oh*
(moon)	(a)	(cube)	(wolf)	(your)

Did you notice any similarity between the words you just read and their English counterparts? You know more than you think! It's important to see how much the two languages share. Remember that a lot of English derives from Latin. It helps to make associations with familiar words. Each time you do this, you are creating a bridge from one shore to another. For example, the word *luna* (moon) comes from Latin as we see in the English word *lunatic*. It was once believed that "lunacy" came from the full moon. All sorts of associations can be made to "illuminate" (in Italian, *illuminare*) these connections.

Consonants

Table 1.4 contains a list of consonants and includes letters recognized in foreign languages. The *R* is capitalized to help remind you to trill. Roll on.

Some letter combinations are more challenging than others because the rules change depending on what vowel is connected to what consonant. By remembering even one word's pronunciation that follows a given rule, you can always fall back on that word as a way of checking yourself; for example, the word *ciao* has a letter combination of *c + i*. Whenever you see similar combinations, such as with the word *cinema*, you'll know how it should be pronounced (*chee-neh-mah*).

Something Extra

To ask someone how to say something in Italian, say, "Come si dice," and add whatever you want to learn.

Question: Come si dice *ice cream* in italiano? (How do you say ice cream in Italian?)

Answer: Si dice gelato. (You say *gelato*.)

Double Consonants

Anytime you see a double consonant, it is important to emphasize that consonant, or you may be misunderstood. Take a look at a few words whose meanings change when there is a double consonant. As you will see, you *definitely* want to emphasize those double consonants in some cases:

> *casa* (house)/*cassa* (cash register)
>
> *ano* (anus)/*anno* (year)
>
> *pena* (pity)/*penna* (pen)

pene (penis)/*penne* (pens or pasta)

dona (he/she gives)/*donna* (woman)

sete (thirst)/*sette* (seven)

Attenzione!

A single *s* is pronounced like "z" as in the name *Gaza* and the Italian word *casa* (house).

A double *ss* is pronounced like "s" as in the English word *tassel* and the Italian word *passo* (pass).

A single *z* is prounounced like "z" as in the word *zebra*.

A double *zz* is pronounced like "ts" as in the English word *cats* and the Italian word *piazza* (plaza).

Diphthongs

A diphthong is not a teeny-weeny-itsy-bitsy bikini. The term *diphthong* refers to any pair of vowels that begins with one vowel sound and ends with a different vowel sound within the same syllable. You pronounce diphthongs all the time when you say the word for a young human male or "boy" where the *oy* is pronounced *oh-yee*, "about" where the *o* and *u* create the diphthong *ow*, and "feud" where the *e* and *u* create the sound *yoo*. The term literally means "two voices" (*di* = two; *thong* = tongue/voice) and originally comes from Greek.

Italian has many dipthongs, all of which should be pronounced as one sound.

Table 1.4   **Pronouncing Consonants Properly**

Letter	Sound	Example
b	bee	*bambino*
c + a, o, u	hard c (as in *cat*)	*candela*
c + e, i	ch (as in *chest*)	*centro*
ch	hard c (as in *cat*)	*Chianti*
d	dee	*due*
f	effe	*frase*
g + a, o, u	hard g (as in *go*)	*gatto*
g + e, i	jay (as in *jet*)	*gentile*
gli	ylee (as in *million*)	*figlio*
gn	nyah (as in *onion*)	*gnocchi*
h (called *acca*)	silent	*hotel*
j* (called *ee-lunga*)	juh (hard j)	*jazz*
k* (called *kappa*)	kuh (hard k)	*koala*
l	elle	*latte*
m	emme	*madre*
n	enne	*nonno*
p	pee	*padre*
q	kew	*quanto*
r	err (slightly rolled)	*Roberto*
rr	errr (r rolled 2-3 times)	*birra*
s (at the beginning of a word)	ess (as in *see*)	*serpente*
s	zee (as in *busy*)	*casa*
sc + a, o	sk	*scala*
sc + e, i	sh	*scena*
t	tee	*tavola*
v	voo	*vino*
w* (called *doppia vu*)	wuh	*Washington*
x* (called *eex*)	eex	*raggi-X*
y* (called *ipsilon*)	yuh	*yoga*
z	zee	*zebra*
zz	ts	*pazzo*

These letters are recognized in words of foreign origin.

Pronunciation	Meaning
bahm-bee-noh	child, m.
kahn-deh-lah	candle
chen-tRoh	center/downtown
kee-ahn-tee	Chianti (a red wine)
doo-eh	two
fRah-zeh	phrase
gah-toh	cat
jen-tee-leh	kind
feel-yoh	son
nyoh-kee	potato dumplings
oh-tel	hotel
jaz	jazz
koh-ah-lah	koala
lah-teh	milk
mah-dReh	mother
noh-noh	grandfather
pah-dReh	father
kwahn-toh	how much
Roh-beR-toh	Robert
bee-Rah	beer
seR-pen-teh	snake
kah-zah	home
skah-lah	stair
sheh-nah	scene
tah-voh-lah	table
vee-noh	wine
Wash-eeng-tohn	Washington
rah-jee-eeks	X-ray
yoh-gah	yoga
zeh-bRah	zebra
pah-tsoh	crazy

Chapter 2

Nuts and Bolts

In This Chapter

➤ Nouns and Pronouns

➤ Adjectives

➤ Adverbs

➤ Prepositions

➤ Possession

This chapter gives a nuts and bolts approach to comprehending the basic components of the Italian language. An understanding of grammar, verbs and vocabulary is essential to learning any language. Rules help the student make sense of an otherwise chaotic subject that has no real significance until interpreted. Your Italian/English dictionary will be your best friend. Keep it close by and within arm's reach.

Nouns

In Italian, every noun (person, place, thing, or idea) is designated as masculine or feminine and singular or plural. Usually, you can tell both a noun's *gender* and its *number* by looking at the ending.

Something Extra

Some nouns can be either masculine or feminine, such as the words *artista*, *dentista*, *parente* and *turista*. Just change the the article without changing the spelling of the noun. Other nouns, regardless the sex of the person to whom they refer, will always stay the same, such as *la persona*.

Something Extra

In Italian, all nouns have a gender: They are either masculine (m.) or feminine (f.). If a word ends in -*a*, such as *la macchina* (the car), it is generally feminine. If a word ends in -*o*, such as *il parco* (the park) it is masculine. Some words end in -*e* , such as *il cane* (the dog), *il mare* (the ocean) and *la stazione* (the station), requiring memorization. Look at the article in front of the word to determine its gender.

Gender

The gender of a noun affects its relationship with other words in a sentence, including adjectives (a word that describes a noun), and if you learn the definite articles along with the nouns, it is easier for you to form sentences correctly later. The magic word here is *agreement*. Nouns and adjectives must always agree. For example, if we want to say the small cat (*il gatto piccolo*), the adjective small (*piccolo*) must agree in gender with the word cat (*gatto*). We'll get to adjectives later, but keep in mind that they follow the same rules.

Attenzione!

Rules are made to be broken. Despite their gender, some nouns have irregular endings:

Masculine nouns ending in -a:

il clima	the climate
il problema	the problem
il programma	the program

Feminine nouns ending in -o:

la foto (short for *fotografia*)	the photo
la moto (short for *motocicletta*)	the motorcycle
la mano	the hand
la radio	the radio

More is More: Making Plurals

In English, add an -s and you have more than one. In Italian, the ending must always reflect the number and gender of the noun. Table 2.1 illustrates how the endings change in the plural.

Table 2.1   Noun Endings

Singular Ending		Plural Ending	Singular Noun		Plural Noun
-o	→	-i	ragazzo	→	ragazzi
-a	→	-e	donna	→	donne
-ca	→	-che	amica	→	amiche
-e	→	-i	cane	→	cani

Attenzione!

Some nouns change into their opposite gender in the plural. Don't try to figure it out. I didn't make the rules.

l'uovo (the egg) → *le uova* (the eggs)

il braccio (the arm) → *le braccia* (the arms)

il dito (the finger) → *le dita* (the fingers)

la mano (the hand) → *le mani (the hands)*

An Article Is Not What You Read in a Newspaper

The term *noun marker* refers to an article or adjective that tells us whether a noun is *masculine* (m.) or *feminine* (f.), *singular* (s.) or *plural* (p.). The noun markers listed in Table 2.2 show the indefinite articles expressing "a," "an," or "one." Table 2.3 shows definite articles expressing "the."

Table 2.2 Indefinite Articles

	Masculine	Feminine
a, an, one	un, uno	una, un'

An Indefinite Article (A, An)

Remember that the indefinite article is only used before *singular* nouns.

Masculine:

> **Un** is used before all singular masculine nouns beginning with either a consonant or a vowel, such as *un palazzo* (a building), *un signore* (a gentleman), and *un animale* (animal), except those nouns beginning with a *z* or an *s* followed by a consonant.

> **Uno** is used just like the definite article *lo*, before singular masculine nouns beginning with a *z* or an *s* followed by a consonant, such as *uno zio* (an uncle) and *uno stadio* (a stadium).

Feminine:

> **Una** is used before any feminine noun beginning with a consonant, such as *una farfalla* (a butterfly), *una storia* (a story), and *una strada* (a street).

> **Un'** is the equivalent of "an" in English and is used before all feminine nouns beginning with a vowel, such as *un'italiana* (an Italian woman), *un'amica* (a friend), and *un'opera* (an opera).

The Definite Articles

Table 2.3   The Definite Articles

	Masculine			Feminine	
	Singular		**Plural**	**Singular**		**Plural**
(The)	lo, l'	→	gli*	la, l'	→	le
	il	→	i			

* Note that the definite article gli is pronounced like ylee.

Singular Definite Articles

Lo is used in front of all singular, masculine nouns that begin with a *z* or an *s* followed by a consonant, such as *lo zio* (the uncle), *lo studio* (the study), and *lo sci* (the ski/skiing).

Il is used in front of all singular, masculine nouns, such as *il ragazzo* (the boy), *il sole* (the sun), and *il vino* (the wine).

L' is used in front of all singular nouns, both masculine and feminine, that begin with a vowel, such as *l'uomo* (the man), *l'opera* (the opera), and *l'atleta* (the female athlete).

La is used in front of all other singular, feminine nouns, such as *la ragazza* (the girl), *la musica* (the music), and *la luna* (the moon).

Plural Definite Articles

Gli is used in front of all plural, masculine nouns beginning with *z* or an *s* followed by a consonant and plural, masculine nouns beginning with a vowel, such as *gli studenti* (the students), *gli zii* (the uncles), *gli animali* (the animals), *gli amici* (the friends).

I is used in front of plural, masculine nouns beginning with all other consonants, such as *i ragazzi* (the boys), *i libri* (the books) and *i gatti* (the cats).

Le is used in front of all plural, feminine nouns, such as *le ragazze* (the girls), *le donne* (the women), *le automobili* (the cars).

The Object Pronouns

An object pronoun replaces the object in a sentence. Because there is no neuter in Italian, all object pronouns must reflect gender and plurality.

Direct and indirect object pronouns replace objects in order to avoid repetition, as in the following examples:

Direct Object Example:

> Kim eats **an apple**. → She eats **it**.

Indirect Object Example:

> Sandro writes **to his parents**. → Sandro writes **to them**.

Table 2.4   Direct and Indirect Object Pronouns

Direct Object Pronouns		Indirect Object Pronouns	
Pronoun	Meaning	Pronoun	Meaning
mi	me	**mi**	to/for me
ti	you (familiar)	**ti**	to/for you
lo	him/it	**gli**	to/for him
la	her/it	**le**	to/for her
La	You (formal)	**Le**	to/for You (formal)
ci	us	**ci**	to/for us
vi	you (plural)	**vi**	to/for you (plural)
li	them (m. and f.)	**loro**	to/for them
le	them (f.)	**(gli)**	to/for them (spoken language)*

Note: Gli is commonly used to replace loro primarily in the spoken language. Although it is not considered correct grammar, it is widely used.

What sometimes makes the object pronouns confusing for the non-native speaker is their similarity to each other as well as to the articles and other words in Italian. This is why it is so important to listen to the context of a sentence. One trick is to remember that direct and indirect object pronouns are all the same *except in the third person singular and plural forms.*

The following rules will make it easier to know when you should use object pronouns:

All object pronouns agree in gender and number with the nouns they replace and are usually placed immediately before a conjugated verb.:

> **Direct Object Pronoun:**
>
> *Lo vedo ogni giorno.* I see **him** every day.
> *(mio fratello)* (my brother)
>
> **Indirect Object Pronoun:**
>
> *Gli offro una mano.* I offer (to) **him** a hand.
> *(a miofratello)* (to my brother)

When the infinitive depends on the verbs *dovere* (to have to), *volere* (to want), or *potere* (to be able to), the object pronoun can also be attached to the infinitive:

> *Voglio accompagnarti* I want to accompany
> *al cinema.* **you** to the movies.

Tall, Dark, and Handsome: Adjectives

Adjectives describe the world we live in. They are pretty, ugly, big, little, black, white, young, old and all of what's in between. Adjectives must agree in gender and number with the nouns they describe and follow the same rules as nouns; feminine adjectives usually end in *-a* and masculine adjectives end in *-o*. Some end in *-e*. Table 2.5 shows you how the singular adjective endings change in the plural.

Table 2.5   Adjectives and Their Endings

Singular Ending		Plural Ending	English Adjective		Italian Adjective
-o	→	-i	famos*o*	→	famos*i*
-a	→	-e	curios*a*	→	curios*e*
-ca	→	-che	magnifi*ca*	→	magnifi*che*
-e	→	-i	intelligent*e*	→	intelligent*i*

Something Extra

In Italian, adjectives must agree in number and gender with the nouns they describe. Generally speaking, masculine nouns use adjectives ending in –o and feminine nouns use adjectives ending in –a. Everyone has to get along, as in *la lingua italiana* or *il dizionario italiano.*

In Chapter 1 you saw many adjectives that are cognates. A few handy adjectives and their opposites are listed in Table 2.6.

Something Extra

Practice using your adjectives wherever you go. Begin with your friends and family. Italians often say, "Che bello!" (or "Che bella!") to describe anything wonderful, whether a meal, a sunset or person.

Table 2.6   **Emotions and Characteristics**

English	Italian	Pronunciation
ambitious	*ambizioso*	ahm-bee-zee-oh-zoh
beautiful	*bello*	beh-loh
blond	*biondo*	bee-ohn-doh
calm	*calmo*	kahl-moh
clever/sly	*furbo*	fooR-boh
courageous	*coraggioso*	koh-Rah-joh-zoh
courteous	*cortese*	koR-teh-zeh
cultured	*educato*	eh-doo-kah-toh
cute/pretty	*carino*	kah-Ree-noh
fat	*grasso*	gRah-soh
funny	*buffo*	boo-foh
generous	*generoso*	jeh-neR-oh-zoh
good	*bravo*	bRah-voh
happy	*allegro*	ah-leh-gRoh
healthy	*sano*	sah-noh
honest	*onesto*	oh-nes-toh
intelligent	*intelligente*	een-tel-ee-jen-teh
kind/polite	*gentile*	jen-tee-leh
loyal	*fedele*	feh-deh-leh
lucky	*fortunato*	foR-too-nah-toh
married	*sposato*	spoh-zah-toh
nice	*simpatico*	seem-pah-tee-koh
organized	*organizzato*	oR-gah-nee-zah-toh
perfect	*perfetto*	peR-feh-toh
proud	*orgoglioso*	oR-goh-lyoh-zoh
romantic	*romantico*	Roh-mahn-tee-koh
sensitive	*sensibile*	sen-see-bee-leh
sincere	*sincero*	seen-cheh-Roh
strong	*forte*	foR-teh
tall	*alto*	ahl-toh
young	*giovane*	joh-vah-neh

English	Italian	Pronunciation
lazy	*pigro*	pee-gRoh
ugly	*brutto*	bRoo-toh
brunette	*bruno*	bRoo-noh
nervous	*nervoso*	neR-voh-zoh
slow/dull	*lento*	len-toh
cowardly	*codardo*	koh-dahR-doh
discourteous	*scortese*	skoR-teh-zeh
ignorant	*ignorante*	ee-nyoh-Rahn-teh
unattractive	*bruttino*	bRoo-tee-noh
skinny	*magro*	mah-groh
boring	*noioso*	noy-oh-zoh
stingy	*tirchio*	teeR-kee-yoh
evil	*cattivo*	kah-tee-voh
sad	*triste*	tRee-steh
sick	*malato*	mah-lah-toh
dishonest	*disonesto*	dee-soh-nes-toh
stupid	*stupido*	stoo-pee-doh
rude	*maleducato*	mah-leh-doo- kah-toh
unfaithful	*infedele*	een-fed-eh-leh
unlucky	*sfortunato*	sfoR-too-nah-toh
divorced	*divorziato*	dee-voR-zee- ah-toh
mean	*antipatico*	ahn-tee-pah- tee-koh
unorganized	*disorganizzato*	dee-soR-gah-nee-zah-toh
imperfect	*imperfetto*	eem-peR-feh-toh
humble	*umile*	oo-mee-leh
practical	*pratico*	prah-tee-koh
insensitive	*insensibile*	een-sen-see-bee- leh
insincere	*bugiardo*	boo-jaR-doh
weak	*debole*	deh-boh-leh
short	*basso*	bah-soh
old	*vecchio*	veh-kee-yoh

Table 2.7 Adjectives and Their Antonyms

English	Italian	Pronunciation
big	*grande*	grahn-deh
clean	*pulito*	poo-lee-toh
complete	*completo*	kohm-pleh-toh
dear/ expensive	*caro*	kah-Roh
first	*primo*	pRee-moh
full	*pieno*	pee-eh-noh
good	*buono*	bwoh-noh
hard	*duro*	doo-Roh
heavy	*pesante*	peh-zahn-teh
hot	*caldo*	kahl-doh
light	*leggero*	leh-jeh-Roh
long	*lungo*	loon-goh
new	*nuovo*	nwoh-voh
next	*prossimo*	pRoh-see-moh
normal	*normale*	noR-mah-leh
open	*aperto*	ah-peR-toh
perfect	*perfetto*	peR-feh-toh
pleasing	*piacevole*	pee-ah-cheh- voh-leh
real	*vero*	veh-Roh
safe/sure	*sicuro*	see-koo-Roh
strong	*forte*	foR-teh
true	*vero*	veh-Roh

English	Italian	Pronunciation
small	*piccolo*	pee-koh-loh
dirty	*sporco*	spoR-koh
incomplete	*incompleto*	een-kohm-pleh-toh
inexpensive	*economico*	eh-koh-noh- mee-koh
last	*ultimo*	ool-tee-moh
empty	*vuoto*	vwoh-toh
bad	*male*	mah-leh
soft	*morbido*	moR-bee-doh
light	*leggero*	leh-jeh-Roh
cold	*freddo*	fReh-doh
heavy	*pesante*	peh-zahn-teh
short	*basso*	bah-soh
used	*usato*	oo-zah-toh
last	*ultimo*	ool-tee-moh
strange	*strano*	stRah-noh
closed	*chiuso*	kee-yoo-soh
imperfect	*imperfetto*	eem-peR-feh-toh
displeasing	*spiacevole*	spee-ah-cheh-voh-leh
fake	*finto*	feen-toh
dangerous	*pericolxoso*	peR-ee-koh-loh-zoh
weak	*debole*	deh-boh-leh
false	*falso*	fahl-zoh

Most Italian adjectives come after the noun, as in *la casa bianca*, or *un viaggio perfetto*.

Buon Viaggio!

The adjective *buono* (good) must change its form in the singular when preceding a noun, as in *È un buon ristorante* (It is a good restaurant) and *Tu sei una buon'amica* (You are a good friend). This adjective must also change in the plural.

Table 2.8   Buono

Gender	Singular	Plural	When It Is Used
Masculine	*buono*	*buoni*	Before s + consonant or z
	buon	*buoni*	Before all other letters
Feminine	*buona*	*buone*	Before all consonants
	buon'	*buone*	Before vowels

Adverbs

Adverbs describe adjectives or verbs and tell how well you do something, such as, "She is *clearly* intelligente." You form many Italian adverbs by adding *-mente* to the end of the feminine form of an adjective, as in "Lei è *chiaramente* intelligente." (chiara + mente = chiaramente). Some adverbs are irregular and need to be memorized. Table 2.9 shows you some of the most important adverbs.

Table 2.9   Adverbs

Adverb	*Avverbio*
a lot, much, very	*molto*
above, on	*sopra*
after	*dopo*

Adverb	*Avverbio*
always	*sempre*
beneath	*sotto*
enough	*abbastanza*
far	*lontano*
here	*qui, qua*
immediately	*subito, immediatamente*
inside	*dentro*
less	*meno*
near	*vicino*
never	*mai*
not very	*poco*
now	*adesso, ora*
often	*spesso*
still, again	*ancora*
then	*allora*
there	*li, la*
too, too much	*troppo*
usually	*di solito*

Fast Forward

Seeing is believing. One of the first things a child learns are the colors. Practice using your colors in Italian the next time you go to the *supermercato*.

arancione (orange)	grigio (gray)
azzurro (sky blue)	marrone (brown)
beige (beige)	nero (black)
bianco (white)	rosa (pink)
blu (blue)	rosso (red)
giallo (yellow)	viola (purple)

Something Extra

In lieu of an adverb, it's possible to use the preposition *con* + a noun:

con allegria → allegramente	*happily*
con attenzione → attentamente	*attentively*
con velocità → velocemente	*quickly*

This and These

The demonstrative pronouns, this and these must always agree with the nouns to which they refer, as in *questo libro* (this book) or *queste case* (these houses).

Table 2.10   This/These

Pronoun	Masculine	Feminine
this	*questo*	*questa*
these	*questi*	*queste*

Prepositions: Sticky Stuff

Prepositions are the glue of a phrase, tying the words together. They show the relationship between a noun and another word in a sentence. Prepositions are highly idiomatic and should be remembered within a context, rather than exclusively memorized.

Table 2.11   Prepositions

Preposition	Italian
about/around (when making an estimation)	*circa*
above	*sopra*
after	*dopo*
against/opposite to	*contro*
around	*attorno a*
before	*davanti a*
behind	*dietro a*
beside	*accanto a*
besides/beyond	*oltre*
between/among	*fra/tra*

continues

Table 2.11 Continued

Preposition	Italian
except/save	*eccetto*
far from	*lontano da*
for/in order to	*per*
from/by	*da*
in front of/before/ahead	*avanti*
inside	*dentro a*
near	*vicino*
of, from, about	*di*
on top of	*su*
outside	*fuori di*
to/at	*a*
under	*sotto*
until/as far as	*fino a*
with	*con*
without	*senza*

Contractions

A contraction, in linguistic terms, is a single word made out of two words. The prepositions in Table 2.12 form contractions when followed by a definite article. Notice that the endings remain the same as the definite article. A contraction can be as simple as *alla* (to the) or *sul* (on the).

Something Extra

The most commonly used prepositions include:

a	(to/at)	*Andiamo a Roma.* (We're going to Rome.)
con	(with)	*Vado con Roberto.* (I am going with Roberto.)
da	(from/by)	*Non ho niente da fare.* (I have nothing to do.)
di	(of/from)	*Di dove sei?* (Where are you from?)
i	(in/to)	*Viaggiamo Italia.* (We are traveling to Italy.)
per	(for)	*Questo regalo è per te.* (This present is for you.)
su	(on)	*Il libro sta sulla scrivania.* (The book is on the desk.)

Table 2.12   Contractions

Preposition	Masculine Singular			Masculine Plural		Feminine Singular		Feminine Plural
	il	lo	l'	i	gli	la	l'	le
a	al	allo	all'	ai	agli	alla	all'	alle
in	nel	nello	nell'	nei	negli	nella	nell'	nelle
di	del	dello	dell'	dei	degli	della	dell'	delle
su	sul	sullo	sull'	sui	sugli	sulla	sull'	sulle
da	dal	dallo	dall'	dai	dagli	dalla	dall'	dalle

Possession

In Italian, the possessive adjectives must always be followed by a noun (my house, your house, and so on). Both the possessor and what is possessed must agree in *gender* and *number*. For instance, if what is being possessed is a feminine, singular noun, such as *la casa*, then the possessive adjective must also be feminine, singular, as in *la mia casa* (my house). It's not enough to determine whose house it is.

Table 2.13 Possessives

Possessive Adjective	Singular		Plural	
	Masculine	Feminine	Masculine	Feminine
my	*il mio*	*la mia*	*i miei*	*le mie*
your	*il tuo*	*la tua*	*i tuoi*	*le tue*
his/her/its	*il suo*	*la sua*	*i suoi*	*le sue*
Your (polite)*	*il Suo*	*la Sua*	*i Suoi*	*le Sue*
our	*il nostro*	*la nostra*	*i nostri*	*le nostre*
your	*il vostro*	*la vostra*	*i vostri*	*le vostre*
their	*il loro*	*la loro*	*i loro*	*le loro*

Notice that the third person singular possessive adjectives sua and suo can mean both his or her, because the possessive adjective agrees with the noun it modifies, not with the subject.

Something Extra

Another way to indicate possession is to use the thing being possessed + the preposition *di* + the possessor.

il libro di Rosetta	(the book of Rosetta; Rosetta's book)
la macchina di Walter	(the car of Walter; Walter's car)

Chapter 3

An Action Packed Adventure

In This Chapter

➤ Subject pronouns

➤ Verb families and conjugation

➤ Asking and answering questions

Verbs are the skeleton of a language. They are words that indicate actions or states of being. The *infinitive* of a verb is simply a verb in its unconjugated form, as in *to eat, to study, to travel.*

Way back when linguists began making sense of the universe of words, they realized that there were only three spheres of existence. "I" can exist, "you" can exist and "he or she" can exist. (In the plural, it's "we," "you," and "they.") The linguists decided to call these *persons*. Look at the subject pronouns in Table 3.1.

Something Extra

If you are unclear as to whether to use the *tu* form or the *Lei* form of the verb, be conservative and use the latter. Otherwise, you may unwittingly offend the person you are addressing.

Table 3.1 Subject Pronouns

Person	Singular	Plural
First	*io* (I)	*noi* (we)
Second	*tu* (you, informal)	*voi* (you, plural)
Third	*lui/lei/Lei* (he/she/You, polite)*	*loro* (they)

The pronoun Lei (with a capital "L") signifies "you" (polite, or formal); the pronoun lei signifies "she." Both, however, are third person.

Italian subject pronouns are used much less than in English because the verb endings usually indicate the subject quite clearly.

All in the Family

There are three kinds of verb families in Italian, *-are*, *-ere*, and *-ire* and each family has its own set of rules. These are called *regular* verbs. Irregular verbs must be memorized because they do not prescribe to a given set of rules.

Conjugating Verbs

To conjugate verbs, drop the infinitive ending from the stem and then add the conjugated endings. Look at the verbs *celebrare* (to celebrate), *scrivere* (to write), *dormire* (to sleep) and *capire* (to understand) in Table 3.2 to see how this works for each verb family.

Attenzione!

There are actually four forms of "you" in Italian:

Tu is used in informal settings with friends and relatives or when adults address children.

Lei is the polite form of you, and is used with strangers and persons in authority and to show respect or maintain a more formal relationship with someone. It is always capitalized to distinguish it from the pronoun *lei*, meaning "she."

Voi is primarily used to address a group of people, although it can still be used as a formal way of addressing an individual, especially in the south.

Loro is used in rare cases when an extreme form of politeness is required, either when addressing a group of people or someone in a high position, such as a president or the pope. It was once used more commonly and can still be heard in old films.

The *-ire* verbs have two forms of conjugation. You will begin to recognize them as you progress. The *-ere* verbs tend to be highly irregular and often do not conform to the regular rules.

Table 3.2 Regular Verb Endings

Subject Pronoun	-are Verbs (Celebrare)	-ere Verbs (Scrivere)
io	celebro	scrivo
tu	celebri	scrivi
lui, lei, Lei	celebra	scrive
noi	celebriamo	scriviamo
voi	celebrate	scrivete
loro	celebrano	scrivono

Table 3.3 Regular -are Verbs

Verb	Pronunciation	Meaning
affittare	ah-fee-tah-Ray	to rent
aiutare	ah-yoo-tah-Ray	to help
alzare	ahl-zah-Ray	to raise/lift up
amare	ah-mah-Ray	to love
anticipare	ahn-tee-chee-pah-Ray	to anticipate/wait
arrivare	ah-Ree-vah-Ray	to arrive
aspettare	ah-speh-tah-Ray	to wait/expect
assaggiare	ah-sah-jyah-Ray	to taste
avvisare	ah-vee-sah-Ray	to inform/advise
baciare	bah-chah-Ray	to kiss
ballare	bah-lah-Ray	to dance
cambiare	kahm-bee-yah-Ray	to change
camminare	kah-mee-nah-Ray	to walk
cenare	cheh-nah-Ray	to dine
cercare	cheR-kah-Ray	to look for something/to search
chiamare	kee-ah-mah-Ray	to call
comprare	kohm-pRah-Ray	to buy
comunicare	koh-moo-nee-kah-Ray	to communicate
contare	kohn-tah-Ray	to count

-ire Verbs I (Dormire)	-ire Verbs II (Capire)
dormo	capisco
dormi	capisci
dorme	capisce
dormiamo	capiamo
dormite	capite
dormono	capiscono

Verb	Pronunciation	Meaning
conversare	kohn-veR-sah-Ray	to converse
costare	koh-stah-Ray	to cost
cucinare	koo-chee-nah-Ray	to cook
desiderare	deh-zee-deh-Rah-Ray	to desire
domandare	doh-mahn-dah-Ray	to question
eliminare	eh-lee-mee-nah-Ray	to eliminate
entrare	ehn-tRah-Ray	to enter
festeggiare	feh-steh-jah-Ray	to celebrate
formare	foR-mah-Ray	to form/create
fumare	foo-mah-Ray	to smoke
funzionare	foon-zee-oh-nah-Ray	to function
giocare	joh-kah-Ray	to play a game
guardare	gwahR-dah-Ray	to look at something
guidare	gwee-dah-Ray	to drive
imparare	eem-pah-Rah-Ray	to learn
informare	een-foR-mah-Ray	to inform
invitare	een-vee-tah-Ray	to invite
lasciare	lah-shah-Ray	to leave something
lavare	lah-vah-Ray	to wash

continues

Table 3.3 Continued

Verb	Pronunciation	Meaning
lavorare	lah-voh-Rah-Ray	to work
mandare	mahn-dah-Ray	to send
mangiare	mahn-jah-Ray	to eat
misurare	mee-soo-Rah-Ray	to measure
nuotare	nwoh-tah-Ray	to swim
occupare	oh-koo-pah-Ray	to occupy
ordinare	oR-dee-nah-Ray	to order
organizzare	oR-gah-nee-zah-Ray	to organize
osservare	oh-seR-vah-Ray	to observe
pagare	pah-gah-Ray	to pay
parlare	paR-lah-Ray	to speak
partecipare	paR-teh-chee-pah-Ray	to participate
passare	pah-sah-Ray	to pass
pensare	pen-sah-Ray	to think
perdonare	peR-doh-nah-Ray	to forgive/pardon
pesare	peh-zah-Ray	to weigh
portare	poR-tah-Ray	to bring/carry/wear
pranzare	pRahn-zah-Ray	to eat lunch/to dine
pregare	pReh-gah-Ray	to pray/request
prenotare	pReh-noh-tah-Ray	to reserve
preparare	pReh-pah-Rah-Ray	to prepare
pronunziare	pRoh-noon-zee-ah-Ray	to pronounce
provare	pRoh-vah-Ray	to try
raccontare	Rah-kohn-tah-Ray	to tell/recount
riparare	Ree-pah-Rah-Ray	to repair/fix
rispettare	Ree-speh-tah-Ray	to respect
ritornare	Ree-toR-nah-Ray	to return
scambiare	skahm-bee-ah-Ray	to exchange
scusare	skoo-zah-Ray	to excuse
soddisfare	soh-dee-sfah-Ray	to satisfy
spiegare	spee-yeh-gah-Ray	to explain

Verb	Pronunciation	Meaning
sposare	spoh-zah-Ray	to marry
stare	stah-Ray	to be/stay
studiare	stoo-dee-ah-Ray	to study
telefonare	teh-leh-foh-nah-Ray	to telephone
terminare	teR-mee-nah-Ray	to terminate
toccare	toh-kah-Ray	to touch
trovare	tRoh-vah-Ray	to find
usare	oo-zah-Ray	to use
verificare	veh-Ree-fee-kah-Ray	to verify
viaggiare	vee-ah-jah-Ray	to travel
visitare	vee-zee-tah-Ray	to visit

Table 3.4   Regular -ere Verbs

Verb	Pronunciation	Meaning
accendere	ah-chen-deh-Ray	to light/turn on
assistere	ah-see-steh-Ray	to assist
attendere	ah-ten-deh-Ray	to attend/to wait for
cadere	kah-deh-Ray	to fall
chiedere	kee-eh-deh-Ray	to ask
chiudere	kee-oo-deh-Ray	to close
conoscere	koh-noh-sheh-Ray	to know (someone)
consistere	kohn-see-steh-Ray	to consist
correre	koh-Ray-Ray	to run
credere	kReh-deh-Ray	to believe
cuocere	kwoh-cheh-Ray	to cook
decidere	deh-chee-deh-Ray	to decide
descrivere	deh-skRee-veh-Ray	to describe
dipendere	dee-pen-deh-Ray	to depend
discutere	dee-skoo-teh-Ray	to discuss

continues

Table 3.4 Continued

Verb	Pronunciation	Meaning
dividere	dee-vee-deh-Ray	to divide
esistere	eh-zee-steh-Ray	to exist
esprimere	eh-spree-meh-Ray	to express
godere	goh-deh-Ray	to enjoy
includere	een-kloo-deh-Ray	to include
insistere	een-see-steh-Ray	to insist
leggere	leh-jeh-Ray	to read
mettere	meh-teh-Ray	to put/place/set
muovere	mwoh-veh-Ray	to move
nascondere	nah-skohn-deh-Ray	to hide
offendere	oh-fen-deh-Ray	to offend
perdere	peR-deh-Ray	to lose
permettere	peR-meh-teh-Ray	to permit
prendere	pRen-deh-Ray	to take
ricevere	Ree-cheh-veh-Ray	to receive
riflettere	Ree-fleh-teh-Ray	to reflect
ripetere	Ree-peh-teh-Ray	to repeat
risolvere	Ree-sohl-veh-Ray	to resolve
rispondere	Ree-spohn-deh-Ray	to respond
scendere	shen-deh-Ray	to descend
scrivere	skRee-veh-Ray	to write
spendere	spen-deh-Ray	to spend
succedere	soo-cheh-deh-Ray	to happen/occur
uccidere	oo-chee-deh-Ray	to kill
vedere	veh-deh-Ray	to see
vendere	ven-deh-Ray	to sell
vincere	veen-cheh-Ray	to win
vivere	vee-veh-Ray	to live

Table 3.5   Group I: Regular -ire Verbs

Verb	Pronunciation	Meaning
aprire	ah-pRee-Ray	to open
bollire	boh-lee-Ray	to boil
dormire	doR-mee-Ray	to sleep
fuggire	foo-jee-Ray	to escape
offrire	oh-fRee-Ray	to offer
partire	paR-tee-Ray	to depart
seguire	seh-gwee-Ray	to follow
servire	seR-vee-Ray	to serve

Table 3.6   Group II: Regular -ire Verbs

Verb	Pronunciation	Meaning
capire	kah-pee-Ray	to understand
costruire	koh-stroo-ee-Ray	to construct
definire	deh-fee-nee-Ray	to define
diminuire	dee-mee-noo-ee-Ray	to diminish
finire	fee-nee-Ray	to finish
preferire	pReh-feh-Ree-Ray	to prefer
pulire	poo-lee-Ray	to clean
spedire	speh-dee-Ray	to send
suggerire	soo-jeh-Ree-Ray	to suggest
trasferire	tRah-sfeh-Ree-Ray	to transfer

Making Sentences

It's very easy to make sentences in Italian. One of the few differences between English and Italian involves the placement of adjectives and adverbs, which generally come after the noun, as in the sentence, *Capisco la lingua italiana* (I understand the Italian language) or, *Parli bene* (You speak well). Unlike English, most nouns require an article in front of them. For example, "next week" would be *la settimana prossima* (literally, "the week next").

Asking Questions

The easiest way to indicate that you're asking a question is by changing your intonation. All you need to do is raise your voice at the end of the sentence, just like in English. *Capisci?*

Another way to ask a simple yes/no question is to add the tags *vero?* ("true?" or "right?"), *no?*, and *giusto?* ("is that so?" or "is that correct?") to the end of a sentence, such as, "*Noi partiamo alle otto, no?*" (We're leaving at 8:00, no?).

Answering Questions

To answer a question affirmatively (yes), use *sì* and give your response.

To answer a question negatively (no), use *no* attached to **non** before the conjugated verb form. This is equivalent to our "don't" as in, "No, I don't smoke."

(Lei) Fuma le sigarette?	*Sì, fumo le sigarette.*
	No, non fumo le sigarette.

If you are answering a question and starting your sentence with "No," these negative expressions come directly after "No," but before the conjugated verb.

| ***mai*** | never | As in, "*No, non fumo mai.*" |
| ***niente*** | nothing | As in, "*No, non desidero niente.*" |

Tenses

This book will cover the present (*presente*), present perfect (*passato prossimo*) and imperfect (*imperfetto*) tenses while touching on the conditional tense. You may want to consult *The Complete Idiot's Guide to Learning Italian* for a more in-depth understanding of other tenses.

Fast Forward

An easy way to speak of the future is to use the present tense + the time in the future you are referring to, such as *Domani vado al cinema* (Tomorrow I am going to the movies).

Chapter 4

Working the Crowd

In This Chapter

➤ Greetings and salutations

➤ To be: *essere* versus *stare*

➤ There is/there are

➤ Professions

➤ Family members

➤ The verb *avere*

➤ Countries and nationalities

If you're too shy to talk, you'll never speak Italian. The only way you're going to learn to *comunicare* is by shedding your inhibitions and putting yourself out there. Small talk may not be your idea of a good time, but it's a start. You can get into the deeper meaning of life in later chapters. For now, you'll learn a few conversation openers and how to tell people a little about yourself.

Table 4.1 Greetings and Salutations

English	Italian	Pronunciation
Hello; good day.	*Buon giorno.*	bwon joR-noh
Good evening;	*Buona sera.*	bwoh-nah seh-Rah
Good night/Goodbye.	*Buona notte.*	bwoh-nah not-teh
Mr./Sir	*Signore*	see-nyoh-Ray
Mrs./Ms.	*Signora*	see-nyoh-Rah
Miss	*Signorina*	see-nyoh-Ree-nah
How are you?	*Come sta?*	koh-meh stah
Very well.	*Molto bene.*	mohl-toh beh-neh
Not bad.	*Non c'è male.*	nohn cheh mah-leh
Pretty well.	*Abbastanza bene.*	ah-bah-stahn-zah beh-neh
What is your name?	*Come si chiama?*	koh-meh see kee-ah-mah
My name is (I call myself)...	*Mi chiamo...*	mee kee-ah-moh
See you soon.	*A presto.*	ah pRes-toh
Excuse me.	*Mi scusi.*	mee skoo-zee
Please.	*Per favore.*	peR fah-voh-Ray
Please.	*Per piacere.*	peR pee-ah-cheh-Ray
Thank you.	*Grazie.*	grah-tsee-yay
You're welcome.	*Prego.*	pray-goh

Once you've had the opportunity to know someone a little better you can use these informal greetings.

Table 4.2 Let's Get Personal

English	Italian	Pronunciation
Hi/Bye-bye!	*Ciao!*	chow
Greetings!	*Saluti!*	sah-loo-tee

English	Italian	Pronunciation
How are you?	*Come stai?*	koh-meh sty
Hello!	*Salve!*	sahl-veh
How's it going?	*Come va?*	koh-meh vah
Things are good.	*Va bene.*	vah beh-neh
Not so good.	*Va male.*	vah mah-lay
Not bad.	*Non c'è male.*	nohn cheh mah-lay
So-so.	*Così così.*	koh-zee koh-zee
See you later.	*Arrivederci.*	ah-Ree-veh-deR-chee
Until later.	*A più tardi.*	ah pyoo taR-dee
Until tomorrow.	*A domani*	ah doh-mah-nee

Something Extra

Ciao is informal for hello and more often for goodbye almost everywhere. The term *salve* is also used in informal greetings. *Arrivederci* literally means "to re-see one another" and is commonly used to say goodbye to friends or colleagues. *ArrivederLa* is used under more formal circumstances.

To Be or Not to Be

There are two *to be* verbs: *stare* and *essere*. When you ask someone *Come stai?* (How are you?), you're using the verb *stare*. When you say, *Lui è molto simpatico* (He is very nice), you're using the verb *essere*. Because the two verbs mean the same thing, the difference between them concerns usage. Both of these important verbs are able to stand on their own, but they can also be used as *helping* or *auxiliary* verbs. They are both irregular and it is a good idea to memorize them *immediatamente*.

Table 4.3   The Verbs Essere and Stare

Subject Pronouns	*Essere*	*Stare*	Meaning
io	*sono*	*sto*	I am
tu	*sei*	*stai*	you are (familiar)
lui/lei/Lei	*è*	*sta*	he/she is; You are
noi	*siamo*	*stiamo*	we are
voi	*siete*	*state*	you are
loro	*sono*	*stanno*	they are

When to use *essere:*

➤ To describe nationalities, origins, and inherent unchanging qualities:

Maurizio è di Verona.	Maurizio is from Verona.
Siamo italiani.	We are Italians.
La banana è gialla.	The banana is yellow.

➤ To identify the subject or describe the subject's character traits:

Voi siete simpatici.	You all are nice.
Michele è un musicista.	Michael is a musician.
Sono io.	It's me.

➤ To talk about the time and dates:

Che ore sono?	What time is it?
Che giorno è?	What day is it?

➤ To indicate possession:

Questa è la zia di Anna.	This is Anna's aunt.
Quella è la mia casa.	That is my house.

➤ For certain impersonal expressions:

È una bella giornata.	It is a beautiful day.
È molto importante studiare.	It is very important to study.

When to use *stare*:

➤ To describe a temporary state or condition of the subject:

Come sta?	How are you?
Sto bene, grazie.	I am well, thanks.

➤ To express location:

Stiamo in città.	We are staying in the city.
Patrizia sta a casa.	Patricia is at home.

➤ In many idiomatic expressions:

Sta attento!	Pay attention!
Sta zitto!	Be quiet!

➤ To form the progressive tenses:

Stiamo andando al cinema.	We are going to the movies.
Sto studiando il mio libro.	I am studying my book.

Something Extra

In Italian, if you want to indicate an action in progress that is happening in this moment, you use the *present progressive* tense, which is formed as follows:

1. Conjugate the verb *stare* to agree with the intended subject.

2. Form the progressive tense for the different verb families using the models below:

studi**are**	studi**ando**	studying
scriv**ere**	scriv**endo**	writing
fin**ire**	fin**endo**	finishing

3. Add the two together as in, *Roberto sta studiando* (Robert is studying).

C'è and Ci Sono (There Is; There Are)

The word *ci* signifies *there*. *C'è* (from *ci è*) and *ci sono* correspond to the English *there is* and *there are*. They state the existence or presence of something or someone:

| *C'è un ristorante buono?* | Is there a good restaurant? |
| *Ci sono molti ristoranti buoni.* | There are many good restaurants. |

To make negative statements, simply add the word *non* in front of the sentence:

| *Non c'è speranza.* | There is no hope. |
| *Non ci sono letti.* | There are no beds. |

Ecco! (Here It Is!)

Ecco is not what you hear when you scream into a canyon. It's very similar to the French *voilà*, meaning, "Here it is! Got it!" Although idiomatic, it is also used frequently to express agreement, as when someone might say, "Now you're talking! Yes, that's right."

Ecco la stazione!	Here's the station!
Eccola!	Here it (the station) is!

Ecco is often used with object pronouns (words that substitute for a noun), such as *"Eccolo!"* (Here it is!).

Chi Sei? (Who Are You?)

You can only go so far with the niceties; it's time to get into the nitty-gritty and talk a little about yourself. Table 4.4 lists several common *professioni*.

Table 4.4 Professions

Profession	*Professione*	Pronunciation
accountant	*contabile*	kohn-tah-bee-leh
actor	*attore*	ah-toh-Ray
actress	*attrice*	ah-tRee-cheh
architect	*architetto*	ahR-kee-teh-toh
artist	*artista*	ahR-tees-tah
banker	*bancario*	bahn-kah-Ree-yoh
cashier	*cassiere*	kah-see-eh-Ray
dentist	*dentista*	den-tees-tah
doctor (f.)	*dottoressa*	doh-toh-Reh-sah
doctor (m.)	*dottore*	doh-toh-Ray
electrician	*elettricista*	eh-leh-tRee-chee-stah
firefighter	*pompiere*	pom-pee-eh-Ray

continues

Table 4.4   Continued

Profession	*Professione*	Pronunciation
hair dresser	*parrucchiere*	pah-Roo-kee-eh-Ray
housewife	*casalinga*	kah-zah-leen-gah
jeweler	*gioielliere*	joh-yeh-lee-yeh-Ray
lawyer	*avvocato*	ah-voh-kah-toh
manager	*amministratore*	ah-mee-nee-stRah-toh-Ray
mechanic	*meccanico*	meh-kah-nee-koh
merchant	*commerciante*	koh-mehR-chahn-teh
musician	*musicista*	moo-zee-chee-stah
nurse	*infermiera*	een-feR-mee-yeh-Rah
photographer	*fotografo*	foh-toh-grah-foh
police officer	*vigile*	vee-jee-leh
professor (f.)	*professoressa*	pRoh-fes-oh-Reh-sah
professor (m.)	*professore*	pRoh-fes-oh-Ray
scientist	*scienziato*	shee-ehn-zee-ah-toh
secretary	*segretaria*	seh-gReh-tah-Ree-ah
student (f.)	*studentessa*	stoo-den-teh-sah
student (m.)	*studente*	stoo-den-teh
teacher	*insegnante*	een-sehn-yahn-teh
waiter/waitress	*cameriere*	kah-meh-Ree-eh-Ray
worker	*operaio*	oh-peh-Rah-yoh
writer (f.)	*scrittrice*	skRee-tRee-cheh
writer (m.)	*scrittore*	skRee-toh-Ray

Who, What, Where

You want to find out who's who, what's happening, and where.

Table 4.5 Getting Information

English	Italian	Pronunciation
who	*chi*	kee
what	*che cosa*	kay koh-zah
how	*come*	koh-meh
of/from	*di*	dee
where	*dove*	doh-veh
why	*perché*	peR-kay
which	*quale*	kwah-lay
when	*quando*	kwahn-doh
how much	*quanto*	kwahn-toh

Blood Is Thicker Than Water

In Italy, one of the first things people will want to know about is your family. Do you have brothers or sisters, nephews or nieces? Take a look at who's who in *la famiglia* in Table 4.6.

Something Extra

When discussing one's "children" of both sexes, Italian reverts to the masculine plural: *figli*. The same goes for friends: *amici*. One's *genitori* (parents) can be simply referred to as *i miei*, coming from the possessive adjective "my" as in "my parents." The word used to describe niece/nephew and granddaughter/grandson is the same: *nipote*.

Table 4.6   Family Members

English	Italian	English	Italian
mother	*madre*	father	*padre*
wife	*moglie*	husband	*marito*
grandmother	*nonna*	grandfather	*nonno*
daughter	*figlia*	son	*figlio*
infant	*bambina*	infant	*bambino*
sister	*sorella*	brother	fratello
cousin	*cugina*	cousin	*cugino*
aunt	*zia*	uncle	*zio*
granddaughter	*nipote*	grandson	*nipote*
niece	*nipote*	nephew	*nipote*
mother-in-law	*suocera*	father-in-law	*suocero*
daughter-in-law	*nuora*	son-in-law	*genero*
sister-in-law	*cognata*	brother-in-law	*cognato*
stepsister	*sorellastra*	step-brother	*fratellastro*
godmother	*madrina*	godfather	*padrino*
girlfriend	*ragazza*	boyfriend	*ragazzo*
fiancée	*fidanzata*	fiancé	*fidanzato*
widow	*vedova*	widower	*vedovo*

Refer back to Chapter 3 to indicate possession, as in, *"Questa è mia madre."*

Attenzione

When speaking of immediate family members, there is no article required before the possessive adjective.

The Haves and the Have Nots

Everyone has something and the verb *avere* (to have) is essential if you want to describe how many brothers and sisters are in your family. Like the verbs *essere* and *stare*, *avere* is an irregular verb and its forms must be memorized. The "h" is always silent and should never be pronounced.

Table 4.7   Avere

Italian	English
io **ho**	I have
tu **hai**	you have
lui/lei/Lei **ha**	he/she has; You have
noi **abbiamo**	we have
voi **avete**	you have
loro **hanno**	they have

The fun doesn't stop here. The verb *avere* is used in many commonly used idiomatic expressions, expressly those that describe your needs and feelings, or, if you dare, to tell someone how old you are, as in *"Ho 33 anni"* (I'm 33 years old).

Table 4.8   Idiomatic Expressions with Avere

Idiom	Meaning
avere bisogno di	to need
avere caldo	to feel hot (literally, to have hot)
avere freddo	o feel cold (literally, to have cold)
avere fame	to be hungry
avere sete	to be thirsty
avere voglia di	to be in the mood

continues

Table 4.8 Continued

Idiom	Meaning
avere male di	to have pain/to be sick
avere paura	to be afraid
avere ragione	to be right
avere torto	to be swrong
avere sonno	to be sleepy
avere ____ anni	to be ____ years old
avere vergogna	to be ashamed
avere l'occasione di	to have the chance
avere l'opportunità di	to have the opportunity
avere la possibilità di	to have the possibility

Attenzione!

Note that the verb *avere* (to have) is used to describe physical conditions, whereas in English, we use "**to be**." Feelings that are expressed with the verb *avere* (to have) are followed by a noun. Feelings that are expressed with the verb *essere* (to be) are followed by an adjective.

The Big, Blue Marble

It's a big world out there. Use *essere* + *di* the name of a country to tell someone where you're from or simply use *Sono* + your nationality. Many countries are called the same in Italian. Table 4.9 shows you those that differ slightly.

Table 4.9 Countries

Country	*Paese*	Nationality	*Nationalità*
Belgium	*Il Belgio*	Belgian	*belga*
China	*La Cina*	Chinese	*cinese*
Denmark	*La Danimarca*	Danish	*danese*
Egypt	*L'Egitto*	Egyptian	*egiziano/a*
England/ Great Britain	*L'Inghilterra/ La Gran Bretagna*	English	*inglese*
Ethiopia	*L'Etiopia*	Ethiopian	*etiope*
Finland	*La Finlandia*	Finnish	*finlandese*
France	*La Francia*	French	*francese*
Germany	*La Germania*	German	*tedesco/a*
Greece	*La Grecia*	Greek	*greco/a*
Ireland	*L'Irlanda*	Irish	*irlandese*
Israel	*L'Israele*	Israeli	*israeliano/a*
Italy	*L'Italia*	Italian	*italiano/a*
Japan	*Il Giappone*	Japanese	*giapponese*
Korea	*La Corea*	Korean	*coreano/a*
Lebanon	*Il Libano*	Lebanese	*libanese*
Libya	*La Libia*	Libyan	*libico/a*
Mexico	*Il Messico*	Mexican	*messicano/a*
Norway	*La Norvegia*	Norwegian	*norvegese*
Poland	*La Polonia*	Polish	*polacco/a*
Portugal	*Il Portogallo*	Portuguese	*portoghese*
South Africa	*Il Sud Africa*	South African	*sud africano/a*
Spain	*La Spagna*	Spanish	*spagnolo/a*
Sweden	*La Svezia*	Swedish	*svedese*
Switzerland	*La Svizzera*	Swiss	*svizzero/a*
Turkey	*La Turchia*	Turkish	*turco/a*
U.S.A.	*Gli Stati Uniti d'America*	American	*americano/a*
Vatican City	*La Città del Vaticano*		*Vaticana*

Fast Forward

Using your atlas, study geography Italian style! All geographical terms, including continents, countries, cities, states, towns, islands, and so on, require the definite article:

l'Italia, la Spagna, la Francia, e la Grecia.

All countries, regions, states, towns, and so on are capitalized.

Nationalities are not capitalized.

The following countries all have the same name (or almost exactly) in Italian. Be sure to pronounce them using Italian phonetics:

Angola	Albania	Algeria
Australia	Antigua	Argentina
Bolivia	Austria	Belize
Canada	Botswana	Bulgaria
Costa Rica	Colombia	Congo
Ghana	Cuba	El Salvador
Guinea	Grenada	Guatemala
India	Haiti	Honduras
Iraq	Indonesia	Iran
Liberia	Kenya	Kuwait
Malesia	Liechtenstein	Madagascar
Pakistan	Nepal	Nicaragua
Russia	Panama	Romania

Senegal	San Marino*	Scandinavia
Somalia	Sierra Leone	Siria
Tunisia	Sudan	Taiwan
Vietnam	Uruguay	Venezuela
Zimbabwe	Zaire	Zambia

*San Marino has the honor of being the longest surviving republic in the world.

It's also easy to figure out which continents are which:

L'Africa	L'Antartide	L'Europa
L'America del Nord	L'Asia	
L'America del Sud	L'Australia	

The Regions

The peninsula now known as Italy was once a cluster of city states. Today, Italy is unified; however, each of its 20 regions still has its own flavor and is run by locally elected officials.

The regions are

L'Abruzzo	La Liguria	La Sicilia
La Basilicata	Le Lombardia	La Toscana
La Calabria	Le Marche	Il Trentino-Alto Adige
La Campania	Il Molise	L'Umbria
L'Emilia-Romagna	Il Piemonte	La Val D'Aosta
Il Friuli-Venezia Guilia	La Puglia	
Il Lazio	La Sardegna	

Chapter 5

At the Airport

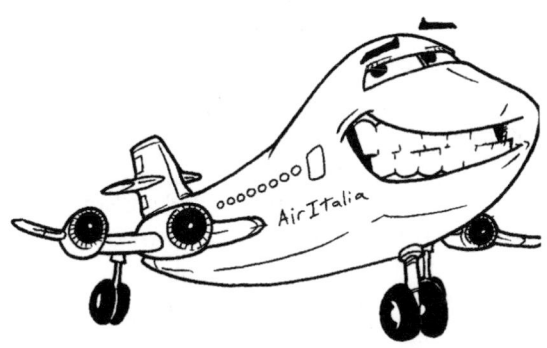

In This Chapter

➤ All about planes and airports

➤ The verb *andare* (to go)

➤ The verb *fare* (to do/make)

➤ How to give and receive directions

➤ Expressing confusion

You're not going to swim to get to Italy—you need to take a plane. Most international flights going to and from Italy communicate with passengers in both English and Italian. This is a wonderful opportunity to develop your listening skills. Instead of relying on your native tongue, pay close attention to the voice coming over the loud speaker when Italian is used. Are you able to grasp the general meaning? The vocabulary in Table 5.1 contains many of the words you might hear.

Table 5.1   Inside the Plane

English	Italian	Pronunciation
airline	*la linea aerea*	lah lee-neh-yah ay-eh-Reh-ah
airplane	*l'aeroplano*	lah ay-eh-Roh-plah-noh
airport	*l'aeroporto*	lah-ay-Roh-poR-toh
aisle	*il corridoio*	eel koh-Ree-doy-oh
to board/embark	*imbarcare*	eem-baR-kah-Ray
emergency exit	*l'uscita d'emergenza*	loo-shee-tah deh-meR-jen-zah
to exit/get off the plane	*salire*	sah-lee-Ray
flight	*il volo*	eel vo-loh
gate	*il cancello*	eel kahn-cheh-loh
landing	*l'atterraggio*	lah-teR-ah-joh
life vest	*il giubbotto di salvataggio*	eel joo-boh-toh dee sahl-vah-tah-joh
non-smoking seat	*un posto per non fumatori*	oon pos-toh peR nohn oo-mah-toh-Ree
on board	*a bordo*	ah boR-doh
row	*la fila*	lah fee-lah
seat	*il posto*	eel poh-stoh
seat belt	*la cintura di sicurezza*	lah cheen-too-Rah dee see-koR-eh-zah
steward/stewardess	*l'assistente di volo*	lah-sees-ten-teh dee voh-loh
take-off	*il decollo*	eel deh-koh-loh
trip	*il viaggio*	eel vee-ah-joh
window	*il finestrino*	eel fee-neh-stRee-noh

On the Inside

You've landed safely and are ushered off the plane toward customs. After your *passaporto* is stamped, many thoughts fill your mind as you grab your bags off the luggage carousel:

You need to find a bathroom, change money, and find out when your connecting flight to Sicily (or Milan, or Pisa) is leaving. Did you lose something *importante* and now need to find the *Ufficio oggetti smarriti* (lost and found)? Table 5.2 gives you all the vocabulary you need.

Fast Forward

Most international airports have signs in both English and Italian. Use the signs as a way of developing your vocabulary as you push your bags through the terminal.

Table 5.2   Inside the Airport

English	Italian	Pronunciation
arrival	*l'arrivo*	lah-Ree-voh
arrival time	*l'ora d'arrivo*	loh-Rah dah-Ree-voh
baggage	*i bagagli*	ee bah-gahl-yee
baggage claim	*la riconsegna bagagli*	lah Ree-kohn-sehn-yah bah-gahl-yee
stop (bus, train, etc.)	*la fermata*	lah feR-mah-tah
car rental	*l'autonoleggio*	low-toh-noh-leh-joh
cart	*il carrello*	eel kah-Reh-loh
connection	*la coincidenza*	lah koh-een-cheh-den-zah
customs	*la dogana*	lah doh-gah-nah
departure	*la partenza*	lah paR-ten-zah
departure time	*l'ora di partenza*	loh-Rah dee pahR-ten-zah
destination	*la destinazione*	lah des-tee-nah-zee-oh-neh

continues

Table 5.2 Continued

English	Italian	Pronunciation
elevator	*l'ascensore*	lah-shen-soh-Ray
information	*l'informazione*	leen-foR-mah-zee-oh-neh
money exchange	*lo scambio*	loh skahm-bee-oh
porter	*il portiere*	eel poR-tee-eh-Ray
reservation	*la prenotazione*	lah pReh-noh-tah-zee-oh-neh
ticket	*il biglietto*	eel bee-lyeh-toh

In addition, the following helpful expressions will at the very least get you to Italy comfortably.

Where is customs?	*Dov'è la dogana?*
Where is the ticket office?	*Dov'è la biglietteria?*
I'd like a seat near the window/aisle.	*Vorrei un posto vicino al finestrino/corridoio.*
I'd like to travel in first/second class.	*Vorrei viaggiare in prima/seconda classe.*
I'd like to order a round-trip ticket.	*Vorrei fare il biglietto di andata e ritorno.*
I'd like to take a plane.	*Vorrei prendere l'aereo.*
I'd like to consign bags in the baggage claim.	*Vorrei consegnare i bagagli al deposito bagagli.*
I'd like to reserve a place.	*Vorrei prenotare un posto.*

Going Crazy: The Verb Andare

The verb *andare* (to go) can come in handy as you make your way out of the airport. This is an irregular verb, so you need to memorize the parts outlined in Table 5.3.

Table 5.3   The Verb Andare (to Go)

English	Italian
I go	io **vado**
you go	tu **vai**
he/she goes; You go	lui/lei/Lei **va**
we go	noi **andiamo**
you go	voi **andate**
they go	loro **vanno**

Things to Do: The Verb Fare

The verb *fare* means "to do/make." In Italian, the verb *fare* is often used similarly to the English verb "to take" and appears in many idiomatic expressions. For example, in Italian, you don't "take a trip," but rather "make a trip" (*fare un viaggio*).

Something Extra

Andare is followed by the preposition *in* when describing means of transportation:

to go by car	*andare in macchina*
to go by bicycle	*andare in bicicletta*
to go by train	*andare in treno*
to go by plane	*andare in aeroplano*

However, when going by foot, the preposition *a* is required:

to go by foot	*andare a piedi*

You also use the verb *fare* to tell the weather or to take a picture, a shower, a walk, or a spin. You can go shopping, pretend, or indicate where something hurts. You'll see this verb a lot—and use it often during your travels. Because it is irregular, you must memorize the different parts in Table 5.4.

Table 5.4   The Verb Fare (to Do/Make)

English	Italian
I do	*io faccio*
you do	*tu fai*
he/she does; You do	*lui/lei/Lei fa*
we do	*noi facciamo*
you do	*voi fate*
they do	*loro fanno*

Table 5.5 contains some idiomatic expressions using the verb *fare*.

Table 5.5   Expressions Using Fare

English	Italian
to take a trip	*fare un viaggio*
to take a walk	*fare una passeggiata*
to take a picture	*fare una fotografia*
to ask a question	*fare una domanda*
to make love	*fare l'amore*
to take a shower	*fare la doccia*
to take a bath	*fare il bagno*
to take a spin	*fare un giro*
to pretend	*fare finta*

English	Italian
to show	*fare vedere*
to go shopping	*fare le spese*
to pack/prepare one's bags	*fare le valigie*
to get gas	*fare benzina*
to give a gift	*fare un regalo*
to fill it up	*fare il pieno*
to hitchhike	*fare l'autostop*

Which Way Do I Go?

The verbs *andare* and *fare* are often used to indicate direction. Instead of telling someone to "take a left and then take a right," you tell them to "*make* a left," or "*go* right." The response you get will probably use the interrogative (or command) form of the verb, which we'll get to shortly.

Take a Left, a Right, Go Straight, and Keep Walking

Being able to ask for directions is easy enough. You can point to your map or you can form a simple question. To start you on the right foot, the verbs in Table 5.6 will help you find your way around town.

Table 5.6 Verbs Giving Direction

Verb	Meaning
andare (irregular)	to go
attraversare	to cross
camminare	to walk
continuare	to continue
fare (irregular)	to make/do/take

continues

Table 5.6 Continued

Verb	Meaning
girare	to turn
passare	to pass
prendere	to take
salire (irregular)	to go up
scendere	to go down
seguire	to follow
stare (irregular)	to stay/be

Something Extra

The following terms can be helpful:

nord = nouth	*a sinistra* = to the left
sud = south	*a destra* = to the right
ovest = west	*diritto* = straight
est = east	

Which One?

Quale means "which" or "what," as in *"Qual è il volo per Milano?"*

Singular	Plural
Quale (which)	*Quali* (which ones)
Qual (in front of *è* (is))	*Quali* (which ones)

Fast Forward

Quale refers to a choice between two or more alternatives. *Che* (what) can be substituted for *quale* in almost any given situation:

Quale (or che) ristorante è il migliore?   Which restaurant is the best?

Dazed and Confused

What do you do if you don't understand the response? Rather than sit there with a dumb look on your face, just have them repeat themselves, but slower this time. Use the following phrases to let people know when you just don't get it.

Excuse me.	*Mi scusi.*
How? (a much nicer way of saying "huh?")	*Come?*
I didn't understand.	*Non ho capito.*
I understood.	*Ho capito.*
I'm lost.	*Sono perso/a.*
Repeat another time, please.	*Ripeti un'altra volta, per favore.*
Speak more slowly, please.	*Parli più lentamente, per favore.*
Speak slowly please, I don't speak Italian well.	*Parli piano, per favore, non parlo bene l'italiano.*

Chapter 6

Things That Go

In This Chapter

➤ Means of transportation

➤ Cardinal numbers

➤ Telling time

➤ Time expressions

One of the most stressful aspects of travel is getting to your destination. When traveling within a *città*, you have a few choices about how you're going to get around. It's best to take advantage of the *economico* and quite efficient modes of public *trasporti*. Walking or cycling is always a terrific way of getting to know the corners of a city that you won't see from inside a bus or taxi—as well as a great way to stay in shape. Or, if you dare, you can rent a car.

Table 6.1 covers all your bases (and wheels):

Table 6.1 Modes of Transportation

English	Italian
bus	*l'autobus*
car	*l'automobile*
bicycle	*la bicicletta*
car	*la macchina*
subway	*la metro*
taxi	*il tassì*
train	*il treno*

Take a Ride

You've already learned the verb *andare* (to go), which you use when you want to indicate "going by car" (*andare in macchina*). The regular verb *prendere* (to take) is particularly useful when using public transportation. Consult Chapter 3 for the regular rules of conjugation.

If You're Going by Train or Bus

Whether you are traveling by *autobus* or *treno*, you'll need to know the following expressions:

Table 6.2 Getting Around

English	Italian
by railway	*per ferrovia*
train station	*la stazione ferroviaria*
ticket	*il biglietto*
round-trip ticket	*il biglietto di andata e ritorno*

English	Italian
one-way ticket	*il biglietto di andata*
ticket counter	*la biglietteria*
schedule	*l'orario*
track	*il binario*
waiting room	*la sala d'aspetto*
connection	*la coincidenza*
first/second class	*prima/seconda classe*
stop	*la fermata*
last stop/end of the line	*il capolinea*

Some commonly used verbs and idiomatic expressions may come in handy. You'll have to conjugate the verbs accordingly:

Table 6.3   Verbs and Idiomatic Expressions

English	Italian
to be late	*essere in ritardo*
to be early	*essere in anticipo*
to be on time	*essere in orario*
to change	*cambiare*
to commute	*fare il pendolare*
to get on	*salire*
to get off	*scendere*
to leave	*partire*
to take	*prendere*
to lose	*perdere*

In the meantime, keep these phrases handy:

I would like a round-trip ticket.	*Vorrei un biglietto di andata e ritorno.*
How much does it cost?	*Quanto costa?*
Where is the bus stop?	*Dov'è la fermata dell'autobus?*
Is there a connection?	*C'è la coincidenza?*
At what times does the train leave?	*A che ora parte il treno?*
On what track does the train leave?	*Su quale binario parte il treno?*

If You're Going by *Tassi*

Unless you're traveling with a metered taxi, it's best to agree upon a fare before you begin your trip to avoid any misunderstanding. If possible, find out what the average taxi fare should be from the airport (or train station) to your hotel. In smaller cities and late at night, it is often necessary to call for a cab. Your hotel or guidebook can tell you what these telephone numbers are. Use the following expressions to tell where you are and where you want to go. Italians use the words *tassì* and taxi:

Where is the nearest taxi stand?	*Dov'è il posteggio di taxi più vicino?*
I need a taxi.	*Ho bisogno di un tassì.*
I'd like to go...	*Vorrei andare...*
Stop here.	*Fermi qui.*
Wait for me.	*Mi aspetti.*

Something Extra

In Italy, public transportation is quite efficient, with buses, trains, and *la metro* (subway) to take you just about anywhere you want to go. It's a good idea to purchase bus tickets at a *cartoleria* or *tabacchi* to keep in your wallet because buses do not accept cash or coins. You can also buy *biglietti* (tickets) at train stations and from automated machines. Once you get onto l'*autobus*, you must validate your ticket by punching it into a small box located on the back of the bus. Hold onto your ticket in case of surprise inspection by stern-faced inspectors. When using *la metro*, you must also buy a ticket from either one of the automated machines or from a ticket booth. It's possible to buy daily, weekly, and monthly tickets.

Renting a Car

Renting a car is easiest from the airport because most of the competitors have booths with English-speaking staff. Often, if you ask for a less expensive alternative, a special rate magically appears. It never hurts to ask. If you find yourself in a small, out-of-the-way town, however, the following phrases will help you get some wheels:

I would like to rent a car.	*Vorrei noleggiare una macchina.*
I prefer a car with automatic transmission.	*Preferisco una macchina con il cambio automatico.*
How much does it cost per day (per week) (per kilometer)?	*Quanto costa al giorno (alla settimana) (al chilometro)?*

How much does automobile insurance cost?	*Quanto costa l'assicurazione per l'auto?*

Attenzione!

If you've decided to rent *una macchina*, carefully inspect it inside and out. Make sure there is *un cricco* (a jack) and *una ruota di scorta* (a spare tire) in the trunk, in case you get a *gomma a terra* (flat tire) and it doesn't hurt to check for any pre-existing damages you could later be charged for.

Table 6.4 gives you the Italian words for car parts and predicaments. You never know—that cherry-red Ferrari you rented could turn out to be a lemon.

Table 6.4   Automobile Parts and Predicaments

English	Italian
battery	*la batteria*
bumper	*il paraurti*
carburetor	*il carburatore*
door handle	*la maniglia*
fan belt	*la cinghia del ventilatore*
fender	*il parafango*
flat tire	*una gomma a terra una ruota bucata*
gas tank	*il serbatoio*
headlights	*i fari*
hood	*il cofano*
license plate	*la targa*

English	Italian
motor	*il motore*
muffler	*la marmitta*
radiator	*la radiatore*
spark plug	*la candela d'accensione*
tail light	*la luce di posizione*
tire	*la ruota*
trunk	*il bagagliaio*
window	*il finestrino*
windshield wiper	*il tergicristallo*

Table 6.5 Inside the Car

English	Italian
accelerator	*l'acceleratore*
air conditioning	*l'aria condizionata*
brakes	*i freni*
gear stick	*il cambio*
glove compartment	*il ripostiglio*
handbrake	*il freno a mano*
horn	*il clacson*
ignition	*l'accensione*
keys	*le chiavi*
radio	*la radio*
rear-view mirror	*lo specchietto*
speedometer	*il tachimetro*
steering wheel	*il volante*
turn signals	*le frecce*

Just in case that wasn't enough, Table 6.6 contains some more useful terms related to the road.

Table 6.6 More Words for the Road Warrior

English	Italian
license	*la patente*
sign	*il segnale*
speed limit	*il limite di velocità*
to be prohibited	*essere vietato*
to break down	*guastare*
to change a tire	*cambiare la ruota*
to check	*controllare*
...the water	*...l'acqua*
...the oil	*...l'olio*
...the tires	*...le ruote*
to drive	*guidare*
to get a ticket	*prendere una multa*
to give a ride	*dare un passaggio*
to obey traffic signs	*rispettare i segnali*
to park	*parcheggiare*
to run out of gas	*rimanere senza benzina*
to run/function	*funzionare*
traffic officer	*il vigile*

Signage

Understanding road signs is essential. Familiarize yourself with these international road signs before getting behind the wheel:

Baby, I Got Your Number

In Italy, you're going to need to be able to count to a million since the Italian currency (*lira*) requires you to be able to understand high numbers. For instance, a cappuccino on average is 2,000 lira (£2.000). (Don't panic; it's only about a buck and a half.) If you want to make a date, tell the time, or find out prices, you need to know numbers.

Fortunately, you don't need to use Roman numerals to do your math. Numbers that express amounts, known as cardinal numbers, are called *numeri cardinali* in Italian. Let the counting begin with Table 6.7.

Attenzione!

Numbers under 100 ending in a vowel, such as *venti* (20), drop the vowel when connected to secondary numbers. Examples are *ventuno* (21), *trentotto* (38), *quarantuno* (41), and so on.

After the number *mille* (1000), *mila* is used in the plural, as in, *due mila* (2000).

Table 6.7 Numeri Cardinali

Number	*Numero*	Number	*Numero*
0	*zero*	27	*ventisette*
1	*uno*	28	*ventotto*
2	*due*	29	*ventinove*
3	*tre*	30	*trenta*
4	*quattro*	40	*quaranta*
5	*cinque*	50	*cinquanta*
6	*sei*	60	*sessanta*
7	*sette*	70	*settanta*
8	*otto*	80	*ottanta*
9	*nove*	90	*novanta*
10	*dieci*	100	*cento*
11	*undici*	101	*centouno*
12	*dodici*	200	*duecento*
13	*tredici*	300	*trecento*
14	*quattordici*	300	*trecento*

Number	*Numero*	Number	*Numero*
15	*quindici*	400	*quattrocento*
16	*sedici*	500	*cinquecento*
17	*diciassette*	1,000	*mille*
18	*diciotto*	1,001	*milleuno*
19	*diciannove*	1,200	*milleduecento*
20	*venti*	2,000	*duemila*
21	*ventuno*	3,000	*tremila*
22	*ventidue*	10,000	*diecimila*
23	*ventitré*	20,000	*ventimila*
24	*ventiquattro*	100,000	*centomila*
25	*venticinque*	200,000	*duecentomila*
26	*ventisei*	1,000,000	*un milione*
		1,000,000,000	*un miliardo*

Something Extra

In numerals and decimals, wherever we use commas, the Italians use periods (and vice versa).

English	Italian
1,000	1.000
.25	0,25

Time Is of the Essence

Time is easy to learn. You need to remember the verb *essere* for asking what time it *is*. You use the verb *sapere* (to know) to ask if someone *knows* the time.

Table 6.8   The Verb Sapere (to Know)

Italian	English
io so	I know
tu sai	you know
lui/lei/Lei sa	he/she knows; You know
noi sappiamo	we know
voi sapete	you know
loro sanno	they know

Fast Forward

The next time you don't know something, shrug your shoulders and say, *Non lo so* (I don't know). No one will know that's about the extent of your Italian and you're off the hook!

You can ask the time in two ways:

> What time is it?   *Che ore sono?*
>
> *Che ora è?*

➤ Use *è* when it is one o'clock, noon or midnight, such as *È l'una* (It's 1:00). For all other times, because there is more than one hour, you must use the plural form of *essere,* as in *Sono le tre* (It is 3:00).

➤ To express time after the hour, use *e* (without the accent, meaning "and") plus the number of minutes past the hour:

It is 4:10.	*Sono le quattro e dieci.*
It is 1:15.	*È l'una e un quarto.*

➤ To express time before the next hour (in English, we say "ten to," "quarter to," and so on), use the next hour + *meno* (meaning less) + whatever time is remaining before the next hour:

It is a quarter to eight. (literally, eight minus a quarter.)	*Sono le otto **meno** un quarto.*
It's ten to one. (literally, one minus ten.)	*È l'una **meno** dieci.*

Something Extra

In Italy, schedules are given in military time. If you are leaving at 2:00 pm, you are told 14:00 hours. This may be tricky at first, so confirm that you have understood correctly by asking if it is a.m. (*di mattino*) or p.m. (*di sera*).

If someone is already wearing a watch and asks you for the time, beware. Otherwise, the following expressions in Table 6.9 will help talk about the time.

Table 6.9 Time Expressions

English	Italian
a second	*un secondo*
a minute	*un minuto*
ago	*fa*
an hour	*un'ora*
a half hour	*un mezz'ora*
in the morning	*di mattino*
in the afternoon	*di pomeriggio*
in the evening	*di sera*
early	*in anticipo; presto*
late	*in ritardo; tardi*
and	*e*
At what time?	*A che ora?*
before 3:00	*prima delle tre*
after 3:00	*dopo le tre*
half past	*e mezzo*
in a while	*fra un po'*
in an hour	*fra un'ora*
on time	*in tempo*
less than	*meno (le)*
since	*da*
see you later	*a più tardi*
see you tomorrow	*a domani*
see you soon	*a presto*

Attenzione!

Be careful of the Italian word *tempo* because the word is primarily used when talking about the weather (as in *temperatura*), not time.

Table 6.10 spells out exactly how to tell the time minute by minute, hour by hour.

Table 6.10   Telling Time

English	Italian
It is 1:00.	*È l'una.*
It is 2:00.	*Sono le due.*
It is 2:05.	*Sono le due e cinque.*
It is 3:10.	*Sono le tre e dieci.*
It is 4:15.	*Sono le quattro e un quarto.*
It is 5:20.	*Sono le cinque e venti.*
It is 6:25.	*Sono le sei e venticinque.*
It is 6:30.	*Sono le sei e trenta.*
It is 7:30.	*Sono le sette e mezzo.*
It is 8:40. (20 min. to 9)	*Sono le nove meno venti.*
It is 9:45. (a quarter to 10)	*Sono le dieci meno un quarto.*
It is 10:50. (10 min. to 11)	*Sono le undici meno dieci.*
It is 11:55. (5 min. to noon)	*È mezzogiorno meno cinque.*
It is noon.	*È mezzogiorno.*
It is midnight.	*È mezzanotte.*

Chapter 7

Hallelujah, You've Made It to the Hotel

In This Chapter

➤ The comfort zone: getting the most from your hotel

➤ First things first: ordinal numbers

➤ How to get what you want with *volere*, *potere*, and *dovere*

Whether you're willing to live on a shoestring or you want the best of the best, this chapter will help you get what you need, when you want it.

Location is everything. Perhaps you want your hotel to be in the heart of the city, close to the action. Maybe you want a place that is slightly off the beaten track. What services are nearby? Use the vocabulary in Table 7.1 to help you find the place that's right for you.

Table 7.1 The Hotel and Nearby

Facilities	Italian	Pronunciation
bar	*il bar*	eel bar
barber	*il barbiere*	eel baR-bee-eh-Reh
cashier	*il cassiere*	eel kah-see-eh-Reh
doorman/concierge	*il portiere*	eel poR-tee-eh-Reh
dry cleaner	*la tintoria*	lah teen-toh-Ree-ah
gift shop	*il negozio di regali*	eel neh-goh-zee-oh dee Reh-gah-lee
gym	*la palestra*	lah pah-leh-stRah
hairdresser	*il parrucchiere*	eel pah-Roo-kee-eh-Reh
hotel	*l'albergo*	lahl-beR-goh
laundry service	*la lavanderia*	lah lah-vahn-deh-Ree-yah
maid	*la cameriera*	lah kah-meR-ee-eh-Rah
parking	*il parcheggio*	eel pahR-keh-joh
room service	*il servizio in camera*	eel seR-vee-zee-oh een kah-meh-Rah
swimming pool	*la piscina*	lah pee-shee-nah
tailor	*la sartoria*	lah saR-toh-Ree-yah

A Room with a View

You might think you want to stand at your window and look at the wonderful chaos that makes Rome such a lively place. Beware: Windows facing the street can often be murder on your rest, especially if you want to sleep in a little. Early morning traffic can be quite merciless on one's ears. After you unpack, maybe you want to take a nice bath to unwind. Don't assume there will be a tub in your room; you must ask. Table 7.2 will help you ask for the kind of room you want with the things you require.

Something Extra

Italy has few laundromats. Generally, you must give your laundry to the hotel or bring it to a *lavanderia* where it will be cleaned and pressed for you. Usually you pay per piece and not by weight. If you want something dry-cleaned, you must bring it to the *tintoria*.

Simply Said

The following simple phrases will help you ask for what you need without breaking out your list of conjugated verbs:

I would like...	*Vorrei...*
I need...	*Ho bisogno di...*
I need...	*Mi serve...*
There are no...	*Non ci sono...*

Table 7.2 Your Room

Amenity	Italian	Pronunciation
a bed	*un letto*	oon leh-toh
a room	*una stanza,* *una camera*	oo-nah stan-zah, oo-nah kah-meh-Rah
a double room	*una doppia*	oo-nah doh-pee-yah
with a double bed	*con matrimoniale*	kohn mah-tRee-moh-nee-ah-leh
a single room	*una singola*	oo-nah seen-goh-lah
with air conditioning	*con l'aria condizionata*	kohn lah-Ree-yah kohn-dee-zee-oh-nah-tah

continues

Table 7.2 Continued

Amenity	Italian	Pronunciation
with terrace	*con terrazza*	kohn teh-Rah-tsah
with private bathroom	*con il bagno privato*	kohn eel bah-nyoh pRee-vah-toh
alarm clock	*la sveglia*	lah sveh-lyah
bathtub	*la vasca da bagno*	lah vah-skah dah bah-nyoh
blanket	*la coperta*	lah koh-peR-tah
blow-dryer	*l'asciugacapelli*	lah-shoo-gah-kah-peh-lee
elevator	*l'ascensore*	lah-shen-soh-Reh
heat	*il riscaldamento*	eel Ree-skahl-dah-men-toh
ice	*il ghiaccio*	eel ghee-ah-choh
key	*la chiave*	lah kee-yah-veh
pillow	*il cuscino*	eel koo-shee-noh
refrigerator	*il frigorifero*	eel fRee-goh-Ree-feh-Roh
safe (deposit box)	*la cassaforte*	lah kah-sah-foR-teh
shower	*la doccia*	lah doh-chah
soap	*il sapone*	eel sah-poh-neh
telephone	*il telefono*	eel teh-leh-foh-noh
television	*la televisione*	lah teh-leh-vee-zee-oh-neh
toilet paper	*la carta igienica*	lah kahR-tah ee-jen-ee-kah
towel	*l'asciugamano*	lah-shoo-gah-mah-noh
transformer	*il trasformatore*	eel tRah-sfoR-mah-toh-Reh

In a pinch, you can use the phrases in Table 7.3 to express yourself and get the information you need. The last thing you want to do is rifle through your *dizionario* while the concierge taps his foot.

Fast Forward

Unless at the front desk, many hotel service people don't speak English, affording you a wonderful opportunity to practice your vocabulary skills. The next time you need something, ask for it in Italian and give yourself a pat on the back.

Table 7.3   Useful Expressions

Expression	L'Espressione
Do you speak English?	*Parla l'inglese?*
I'd like to make a reservation.	*Vorrei fare una prenotazione.*
How much does it cost per day?	*Quanto costa al giorno?*
Is there anything less expensive?	*Non c'è qualcosa più economico?*
Is breakfast included?	*È colazione compresa?*
At what time is check-out?	*Qual è l'ora di partenza?*
Did I receive any messages?	*Ho ricevuto dei messaggi?*
May I leave a message?	*Posso lasciare un messaggio?*
This room is too...	*Questa stanza è troppo...*
...small	*...piccola*
...dark	*...buia*
...noisy	*...rumorosa*
Can I pay with...	*Posso pagare con...*
...cash?	*...contanti?*
...check?	*...assegno?*
...credit card?	*...carta di credito?*

Who's on First?

When you *ordinare* (order) your dinner in a *ristorante*, you start with your *primo piatto* (first course), and then move along to your *secondo piatto* (second course). What do all these things have in common (other than the fact that they all taste really good)? They all use *ordinal numbers*.

Ordinal numbers specify the order of something in a series. It's probably obvious (but in case it's not) that the word *primo* is similar to the English word "primary," *secondo* is like "secondary," and so on and so forth. (Remember: You should always be thinking of like-sounding words in English to help you retain your Italian vocabulary.) Table 7.4 gives you a rundown of the ordinal numbers you need and how to write them in abbreviated form.

Table 7.4   Ordinal Numbers

English	Italian	Masc.	Fem.	Pronunciation
first	*primo*	1º	1ª	pRee-moh
second	*secondo*	2º	2ª	seh-kohn-doh
third	*terzo*	3º	3ª	teR-zoh
fourth	*quarto*	4º	4ª	kwahR-toh
fifth	*quinto*	5º	5ª	kween-toh
sixth	*sesto*	6º	6ª	sehs-toh
seventh	*settimo*	7º	7ª	seh-tee-moh
eighth	*ottavo*	8º	8ª	oh-tah-voh
ninth	*nono*	9º	9ª	noh-noh
tenth	*decimo*	10º	10ª	deh-chee-moh

There are some basic rules for using ordinal numbers in Italian:

➤ Like any adjective, ordinal numbers must agree in gender and number with the nouns they modify. As in English, they precede the nouns they modify. Notice how they are abbreviated, as in 1º (1st), 2º (2nd), and 3º (3rd)—much easier than the English. The feminine abbreviation reflects the ending *-a*, as in 1ª, 2ª, and 3ª.

> *la prima volta (1ª)*   the first time
>
> *il primo piatto (1º)*   the first course

➤ You need to use ordinal numbers whenever you reference a Roman numeral, as in Enrico V (*quinto*) or Papa Giovanni Paolo II (*secondo*).

➤ Unlike in English, dates in Italian require cardinal numbers, unless you are talking about the first day of a month, as in *il primo ottobre*. June 8th is *l'otto (di) giugno* because the day always comes before the month. The use of the preposition *di* is optional. Therefore, it's important to remember that in Italian, 8/6/98 is actually June 8, 1998 (and not August 6, 1998).

Something Extra

In Italian, the word for floor is *piano* (just like the instrument). The *primo piano* (first floor) is actually the floor above the *pianterreno* (ground floor) and equal to what is considered the second floor in the U.S. By the way, the number 13 is considered *buona fortuna*—just the opposite from what one might expect.

Anything Is Possible

Phrases are helpful, but an understanding of verbs is essential if you want to think outside the box. The verbs *volere, potere* and *dovere* are all well worth the energy it takes to learn them.

I Want What I Want! (Volere)

You may have already seen the verb *volere*. When you say, *Vorrei*, you are saying, "I would like." You are using the conditional form because you *would like* to express your wants as delicately as possible. Table 7.5 shows you how to express want, pure and simple.

Table 7.5   Volere (to Want)

Italian	English
io **voglio**	I want
tu **vuoi**	you want
lui/lei/Lei **vuole**	he/she wants; You want
noi **vogliamo**	we want
voi **volete**	you want
loro **vogliono**	they want

I Think I Can, I Think I Can! (Potere)

The verb *potere* is what you use to say you are able to do something. Your "potential" is unlimited, as long as you think you can. One thing to keep in mind, however, as you examine Table 7.6: *Potere* is always used with an infinitive, as in *Posso imparare questa lingua* (I can learn this language).

Table 7.6 Potere (to Be Able to/Can)

Italian	English
io **posso**	I can
tu **puoi**	you can
lui/lei/Lei **può**	he/she/You can
noi **possiamo**	we can
voi **potete**	you can
loro **possono**	they can

I Have to... (Dovere)

The verb *dovere*, outlined in Table 7.7, is what you use to express "to have to," "must," or "to owe." Like the verb *potere*, *dovere* is always used in front of an infinitive, such as when you say, *Devo studiare* (I have to study), except when it is used to mean "to owe."

Table 7.7 Dovere (to Have to/Must/to Owe)

Italian	English
io **devo**	I must
tu **devi**	you must
lui/lei/Lei **deve**	he/she/You must
noi **dobbiamo**	we must
voi **dovete**	you must
loro **devono**	they must

Coulda, Shoulda, Woulda

The verbs *dovere* (to have to), *potere* (to be able to), and *volere* (to want) are often used in the conditional tense. When you *should* do something, you use the verb *dovere*. When you *could* do something, use the verb *potere*. When you *would like* something, use *volere.* These verbs in the conditional are often used with the infinitive form of another verb.

Table 7.8 Dovere, Potere, and Volere

Subject	Dovere (Should)	Potere (Could)	Volere (Would Like)
io	dovrei	potrei	vorrei
tu	dovresti	potresti	vorresti
lui/lei/Lei	dovrebbe	potrebbe	vorrebbe
noi	dovremmo	potremmo	vorremmo
voi	dovreste	potreste	vorreste
loro	dovrebbero	potrebbero	vorrebbero

Chapter 8

Rain or Shine

In This Chapter

➤ The weather

➤ Days of the week and months of the year

➤ Vocabulary for all seasons

➤ What's your sign: the zodiac in Italian

The climate in Italy is generally temperate although high up in the mountains, the temperature can be much cooler. Keep in mind that Rome and New York are on the same latitude although Rome is a few degrees warmer.

The verb *fare* (to do/make) is necessary to talk about the weather, but you'll see the *ci + essere* combination here too, as in *C'è il sole*. (It's sunny.) Some of the information in Table 8.1 might be review, and some is new.

Table 8.1 Weather Expressions

English	Italian
What's the weather?	*Che tempo fa?*
It's beautiful.	*Fa bello.*
It's hot.	*Fa caldo.*
It's cold.	*Fa freddo.*
It's bad.	*Fa brutto.*
It's cool.	*Fa fresco.*
It's sunny.	*C'è il sole.*
It's windy.	*C'è vento.*
It's cloudy.	*È nuvoloso.*
It's humid.	*È umido.*
It's raining.	*Piove.*
It's snowing.	*Nevica.*
There is a storm.	*C'è un temporale.*
What is the temperature today?	*Quanto fa oggi?*
It is ___ degrees.	*Fa ___ gradi.*

Weather or Not

There's a lot more out there than rain, sun, and snow. How about snowflakes? Rainbows? Sunsets and sunrises? If someone says it's raining cats and dogs, you know they mean it's raining very hard. Some of the words and phrases in Table 8.2 will help take your conversation about the weather to a more poetic level.

Table 8.2 Cats and Dogs

English	Italian
air	*l'aria*
avalanche	*la valanga*
calm	*sereno*
Celsius	*grado centigrado*
climate	*il clima*
cloud/ cloudy	*la nuvola/nuvoloso*
dry	*secco*
frost	*la brina*
humid	*umido*
ice	*il ghiaccio*
lightning bolt	*il fulmine/il lampo*
mud	*il fango*
ozone	*l'ozono*
pollution	*l'inquinamento*
rain	*pioggia*
rainbow	*l'arcobaleno*
rainy	*piovoso*
smog	*lo smog*
snow	*la neve*
snow flake	*il fiocco di neve*
sunrise	*l'alba*
sunset	*il tramonto*
the atmosphere	*l'atmosfera*
tropical	*tropicale*

Something Extra

Idioms are the pulse of a language. Try these on for size:

It's dog cold.	*Fa un freddo cane.*
It's wolf's weather.	*Fa un tempo da lupi.*
April, every drop a kiss.	*Aprile, ogni goccia un bacile.*

What's Hot and What's Not

To talk about the temperature, you use the verb *fare* in the third person as you do with the weather.

If someone asks, *Quanto fa oggi?* you may find yourself initially confused. What they're really asking is "How many degrees (*gradi*) are there today?" The word *gradi* is implied.

If it's 20 degrees Celsius, you reply, *Fa venti gradi.* (It's twenty degrees.)

If it's ten below, you say, *Fa dieci sotto zero.*

What Day Is It?

You're having so much fun that you've lost track of the days. Monday, Tuesday...it's all the same. Just don't get too carried away; you don't want to miss your plane home.

Something Extra

In Italy, as in all of Europe, the metric system is used to determine the temperature. To convert Centigrade to Fahrenheit, multiply the Centigrade temperature by 1.8 and add 32.

To convert Fahrenheit to Centigrade, subtract 32 from the Fahrenheit temperature and multiply the remaining number by .5.

Here are some basic temperature reference points:

Freezing: 32°F = 0°C

Room Temperature: 68°F = 20°C

Body Temperature: 98.6°F = 37°C

Boiling: 212°F = 100°C

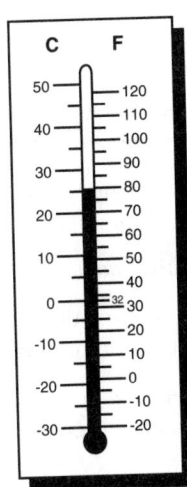

There are few accents in Italian. The days of the week, however, excepting the weekend, all end with what is called the grave accent -ì. When pronouncing days of the week, which are outlined in Table 8.3, always emphasize the last syllable. Note the corresponding planet each day represents. For example, *lunedì* corresponds with *la luna*, as in "moon day." Italians have adopted the English way of expressing the end of the week by using our word "weekend," but you might also hear *la fine della settimana* expressed as well.

Table 8.3 Days of the Week

Day of the Week		Italian
Monday	"moon day"	*lunedì*
Tuesday	"Mars day"	*martedì*
Wednesday	"Mercury day"	*mercoledì*
Thursday	"Jupiter day"	*giovedì*
Friday	"Venus day"	*venerdì*
Saturday	"Saturn day"	*sabato*
Sunday	"God's day"	*domenica*
The weekend	"weekend"	*la fine settimana*

➤ There is no equivalent to the preposition *on* before the names of days:

Arriviamo lunedì.   We are arriving (on) Monday.

➤ You use the definite article in front of a day to describe something you always do:

Andiamo in chiesa   We go to church on Sundays.
la domenica.

Monthly Matters

If you've lost track of the months while you're away, you've been gone for too long. Go home! If, on the other hand, you're planning your next trip, or you want to tell someone when your birthday is, knowing the month is important. Find that special date in Table 8.4.

Table 8.4 I Mesi (The Months)

Month	*Mese*
January	*gennaio*
February	*febbraio*
March	*marzo*
April	*aprile*
May	*maggio*
June	*giugno*
July	*luglio*
August	*agosto*
September	*settembre*
October	*ottobre*
November	*novembre*
December	*dicembre*

➤ Like the days of the week, the months are not capitalized in Italian.

➤ The month always comes after the day and you must always put the definite article in front of the day after which comes the month.

June 25th, 1965 (6/25/65) *Il 25 giugno di 1965 (25.6.65)*

➤ Ordinal numbers are used for the first day of any month.

    June 1st   *Il primo giugno*

The Four Seasons

Ah! What's nicer than springtime in *Toscana* or a beautiful summer day lounging on the beaches of *Sardegna*? How does a bowl of *pasta primavera* sound? Or maybe you would prefer a *quattro stagioni* pizza?

Table 8.5 The Seasons

English	Italian
spring	*la primavera*
summer	*l'estate*
autumn	*l'autunno*
winter	*l'inverno*
season	*la stagione*

Something Extra

To express the notion of being *in* a certain season, the Italians use either the preposition *in* or *d'*:

    Andiamo in Italia   We are going to
    d'inverno.   Italy in the winter.

    In *primavera fa bello.*   It's beautiful in the spring.

Something Extra

If the weather isn't your thing, you can go to another plane and ask someone about their background—astrologically speaking. Find out if you are compatible by asking someone, "*Che segno sei?*" (What's your sign?)

Aries	*ariete*
Taurus	*toro*
Gemini	*gemelli*
Cancer	*cancro*
Leo	*leone*
Virgo	*vergine*
Libra	*bilancia*
Scorpio	*scorpione*
Sagittarius	*sagittario*
Capricorn	*capricorno*
Aquarius	*acquario*
Pisces	*pesci*

Chapter 9

Having Fun

In This Chapter

➤ Sights to see and things to do

➤ The verbs *giocare, uscire, venire, rimanere* and *dire*

➤ How to make suggestions and plans

➤ Exclamations

➤ The verb *piacere*

A lifetime wouldn't be long enough to see all there is in *Italia*. The choices outlined in Table 9.1 are endless. Sometimes it can be a little overwhelming; each *città* has its own charm and specialties. Italy is a country filled with more art from more periods of history than just about any place in the world. Overload is *possibile*, so take it slow and stick with your list of "must-sees," but allow yourself to *scoprire* (discover) something you hadn't anticipated.

Table 9.1 Places to Go

The Place	*Il Luogo*	The Place	*Il Luogo*
the aquarium	*l'acquario*	the museum	*il museo*
the beach	*la spiaggia*	the opera	*l'opera*
the castle	*il castello*	the park	*il parco*
the cathedral	*la cattedrale*	the public square	*la piazza*
the church	*la chiesa*	the sea	*il mare*
the cinema	*il cinema*	the stadium	*lo stadio*
the circus	*il circo*	the theatre	*il teatro*
the discotheque	*la discoteca*	the wine bar	*l'enoteca*
the fountain	*la fontana*	the winery	*l'azienda vinicola*
the garden	*il giardino*	the zoo	*lo zoo*
the market	*il mercato*		

One of the most beautiful words in any language is the word *vacation*. But what are you going to do when you're on your holiday? Table 9.2 contains a few expressions and some vocabulary related to trip-taking that will enhance your fabulous Italian experience. As usual, you'll have to conjugate the verb to refer to the subject, as in, *Andiamo al mare* (We're going to the seashore).

Table 9.2 Things to Do

English	Italian
to be on vacation	*essere in ferie*
to be on vacation	*essere in vacanza*
to go camping	*fare il campeggio*
to go to the country	*andare in campagna*
to go to the mountains	*andare in montagna*

English	Italian
to go to the seashore	*andare al mare*
to party/celebrate	*festeggiare*
to take a cruise	*fare una crociera*
to take a spin/tour	*fare un giro*
to take a trip	*fare un viaggio*
to take a vacation	*fare una vacanza*

Something Extra

Ferragosto refers to the month of August, when most Italians pack up and head toward *il mare* or *le montagne* for their vacations. Generally lasting through the month, if you should find yourself in Italy during this *periodo*, don't be surprised to find many of the smaller stores closed for *le ferie* (the holidays).

Name Your Game

Don't get confused when you hear the word *futball*. It means soccer, also known as *il calcio*. Someone once said that there are three things you should never dare take away from an Italian: *la mamma*, *la pasta*, and *il calcio*. Expect anarchy if you dare. Many sports require the use of the verbs *fare* and *andare*.

Table 9.3   Game Time

Sport	*Lo Sport*
aerobics	*l'aerobica*
baseball	*il baseball*
basketball	*la pallacanestra*
bicycling	*andare in bicicletta*
boating	*andare in barca*
diving	*fare il subacqueo*
fishing	*pescare*
football	*il football americano*
game	*la partita*
golf	*il golf*
hockey	*l'hockey*
horseback riding	*andare a cavallo*
jogging	*fare footing*
karate	*fare karate*
rock climbing	*l'alpinismo*
inline skating	*fare pattinaggio*
rowing	*il canottaggio*
skating	*pattinare*
skiing	*lo sciare*
soccer	*il calcio*
surfing	*fare il surf*
swimming	*fare il nuoto, nuotare*
team	*la squadra*
tennis	*il tennis*
volleyball	*la pallavolo*
wind surfing	*il windsurf*

Something Extra

The verb *giocare* (to play) is used for playing games. Rainy days and blistered feet are perfect occasions for getting out that portable backgammon set.

The Game	Il Gioco
backgammon	*il backgammon*
briscola (a popular card game)	*la briscola*
cards	*le carte*
checkers	*la dama*
chess	*gli scacchi*
dice	*i dadi*
gambling	*giocare d'azzardo*
hide-and-seek	*Cu-cù*
poker	*il poker*
scopa (a popular card game)	*scopa*
solitaire	*il solitario*
tarot	*i tarocchi*

Instant Italian

Okay, you want it all spelled out. You don't have the *pazienza* to worry about conjugating verbs. Just say:

Do you have a map of the city?	*Avete una pianta della città?*
At what time does it open?	*A che ora si apre?*
At what times does it close?	*A che ora si chiude?*

How much is the admission?	*Quanto costa per entrare?*
May I take pictures?	*Posso fare le foto?*
How do I get there?	*Come si arriva?*

More Irregular Verbs

There are a few more verbs you should learn before you strap on a camera and put on those walking shoes. You've already learned a few of the irregular verbs like *andare* and *fare*. By now, you should have the subject pronouns memorized, especially the *Lei* form (you, polite).

Giocare

You're no party pooper. Let the games begin!

Attenzione!

The verb *giocare* is pronounced *joh-kah-Reh* and the conjugations always maintain the hard k sound.

Lest you not get confused, there is another verb meaning to play: *suonare.* This verb is used when you are playing a musical instrument and literally means to make sound.

Table 9.4 The Verb Giocare (to Play)

Italian	English
io **gioco**	I play
tu **giochi**	you play
lui/lei/Lei **gioca**	he/she plays; You play

Italian	English
noi **giochiamo**	we play
voi **giocate**	you play
loro **giocano**	they play

Uscire

You're ready to paint the town red and you're dying to go out. *Uscire*, which is fully conjugated in Table 9.5, will get you out of your hotel room and into the heart of where the action is. By the way, you'll see this verb used above any exit: *Uscita*.

Something Extra

Remember your pronunciation rules: *sco* is pronounced like *sk* in the word "sky." *sci* is pronounced like *sh* in the word "she."

Table 9.5 The Verb Uscire (to Go Out/Exit)

Italian	English
io **esco**	I go out
tu **esci**	you go out
lui/lei/Lei **esce**	he/she goes out; You go out
noi **usciamo**	we go out
voi **uscite**	you go out
loro **escono**	they go out

Venire

You don't know if you're coming or going. Try this one on for size:

Table 9.6   The Verb Venire (to Come)

Italian	English
io **vengo**	I come
tu **vieni**	you come
lui/lei/Lei **viene**	he/she comes; You come
noi **veniamo**	we come
voi **venite**	you come
loro **vengono**	they come

Rimanere

You've fallen in love and have decided to remain in Italy. This verb will come in handy:

Table 9.7   The Verb Rimanere (to Remain)

Italian	English
io **rimango**	I remain
tu **rimani**	you remain
lui/lei/Lei **rimane**	he/she remains; You remain
noi **rimaniamo**	we remain
voi **rimanete**	you remain
loro **rimangono**	they remain

Dire

The verb *dire* (to say/tell) is irregular but it is a good verb to know:

Table 9.8 The Verb Dire (to Say/Tell)

Italian	English
*io **dico***	I say
*tu **dici***	you say
*lui/lei/Lei **dice***	he/she says; You say
*noi **diciamo***	we say
*voi **dite***	you say
*loro **dicono***	they say

Che Bello!

A few exclamations, as shown in Table 9.9, might come in handy when you're truly moved or utterly disgusted.

Table 9.9 Exclamations

Expression	*L'Espressione*
How beautiful!	*Che bello!*
How ugly!	*Che brutto!*
What a disaster!	*Che disastro!*
Excellent!	*Eccellente!*
Fantastic!	*Fantastico!*
Fabulous!	*Favoloso!*
Magnificent!	*Magnifico!*
Marvelous!	*Meraviglioso!*
Horrible!	*Orribile!*
Ridiculous!	*Ridicolo!*
Stupendous!	*Stupendo!*
Terrible!	*Terribile!*

Something Extra

Here are 15 "must sees" according to Wendy Keyes at the Film Society of Lincoln Center, New York City.

The White Sheik (Fellini)	The Conformist (Bertolucci)
Bicycle Thief (De Sica)	Ossessione (Visconti)
Roma: Open City (Rossellini)	La Dolce Vita (Fellini)
Kaos (Taviani Brothers)	Seven Beauties (Wertmuller)
Caro Diario (Moretti)	Hands Over the City (Rosi)
The Human Voice (Rossellini)	L'Avventura (Antonioni)
L'Amerika (Amelio)	Before the Revolution (Bertolucci)
Big Deal on Madonna Street (Monicelli)	

The Power of Suggestion

Rather than tell someone what you want to do, there's a more subtle way; you can suggest by dropping a couple of hints, such as "Why don't we take a trip?" or "Why don't you go jump in a lake?"

➤ The easiest way to make a suggestion is to ask this simple question using the words *perche non...* (why not...):

Perché non + the verb in the second person plural form (noi)?

For example:

Perché non andiamo Italia?	Why don't we go to Italy?
Perché non partiamo domani?	Why don't we leave tomorrow?

➤ If you want to let your easy-going friend think he or she actually has a choice in the matter, you can ask them what they think of the idea.

Che ne pensi?	What do you think (of it)?
Che ne dici?	What do you say (about it)?

Something Extra

The pronoun *ne* is used in a variety of situations, most of which are idiomatic. *Ne* can be translated to mean some, any, of it, of them, some of them, any of it and any of them. It is primarily used to refer to a subject that has already been mentioned.

➤ To suggest the English "Let's," use the second person plural form (noi):

Andiamo a mangiare.	Let's go eat.
Mangiamo.	Let's eat.

Useful Phrases Expressing Suggestion

Without getting into a lot of grammatical gobbly-gook, you can shape all of the following to whatever you want to suggest doing. The second column shows you what verb is used. Just add the infinitive of any verb you want to use after each expression.

Table 9.10   Getting Suggestive

Familiar	Polite	English
Ti va di...? (tu)	Le va di...? (Lei)	(**andare**) Are you in the mood to...? (idiomatic; literally, does it go with you?)
Ti interessa...? (tu)	Le interessa...? (Lei)	(**interessare***) Are you interested in...? (literally, is it interesting to you?)
Ti piacerebbe...? (tu)	Le piacerebbe...? (Lei)	(**piacere***-conditional) Would you like...? (literally, would it please you to...?)

*Note: Both these verbs require the use of object pronouns.

Yes or No

Rebellious teenagers give abrupt yes or no answers to questions. Most of the rest of us say, "Yes, but..." or "No, because..." If you want to elaborate on your answer, here's what you have to do: Change the pronoun *Le* or *ti* from the question to *mi* in your answer. Check out the following examples:

Table 9.11 Elaborating

Affirmativo	Negativo
Sì, mi va di andare al cinema.	No, non mi va di andare al cinema.
Sì, mi interessa fare un viaggio in Italia.	No, non mi interessa fare un viaggio in Italia.
Sì, mi piacerebbe vedere il castello.	No, non mi piacerebbe vedere il castello.

What's Your Pleasure? The Verb Piacere

There is no verb "to like" in Italian. You must always use *piacere* (to be pleasing to). Instead of "I like chocolate," you say, "Chocolate is pleasing to me." In Italian, the subject of the verb (that which determines which person should be used), is the thing that is liked. This is quite different from English. You'll need to know your indirect object pronouns to use this verb.

Something Extra

The indirect object pronouns are used with the verb *piacere*, as in, *Gli piacciono i dolci* (sweets are pleasing to him).

Singular	Plural
mi (to/for me)	*ci* (to/for us)
ti (to/for you)	*vi* (to/for you)
gli/ le/ Le (to/for him/her/You)	*loro* (to/for them)

Piacere is rarely used in anything other than the third person singular and plural. See how it conjugates:

> *Piace* (it is pleasing)   *Piacciono* (they are pleasing)

Some rules about the verb *piacere:*

Piacere is almost always used in third person (singular and plural) and is always used with an indirect object or indirect object pronoun (to me, to you, to him/her, to us, to them):

> *Ti piace la cioccolata?*   Do you like chocolate?; Is chocolate pleasing to you?
>
> *Sì, mi piacciono i cioccolatini.*   Yes, I like chocolates; Yes, chocolates are pleasing to me.

If the subject is an infinitive, it is considered singular:

> *Ti piace mangiare la cioccolata?*   Do you like to eat chocolate; is eating chocolate pleasing to you?
>
> *Sì, mi piace mangiare la cioccolata.*   Yes, I like to eat chocolate.

Attenzione!

The verb *dispiacere* means "to be sorry" as well as "to mind." It is used exactly like the verb *piacere:*

> *Mi dispiace.*   I'm sorry.
>
> *Le dispiace attendere un momento?*   Do you mind holding for a moment?

Chapter 10

Shop 'Til You Drop

Italy is a place you definitely want to shop. While you're there, you may also have particular needs, such as a new battery for your camera or a little touch-up on those gray roots. Whatever your *esigenze* (needs), this chapter will give you all the *vocabolario* necessary to get you what you want, when you want

The following sentences in Table 10.1 will help you find out *if* someone can help you, *when* they are open, *how* to get there, and *what* your needs are.

Table 10.1   Help!

The Phrase	*La Frase*
I need...	*Ho bisogno di...*
Can you help me?	*Mi potete aiutare?*
Are you open	*Siete aperti*
...now?	*...adesso?*
...until what time?	*...fino a che ora?*
...Sundays?	*...la domenica?*
Where is...?	*Dov'è...?*
Do you have...?	*Avete...?*
Are you able to...?	*Potete...?*
Do you know...	*Conosce...*
...a good hairdresser?	*...un buon parrucchiere?*
...a good tailor?	*...un buon sarto?*
...a good shoemaker?	*...un buon calzolaio?*
...a good dry cleaner?	*...una buona tintoria?*

Stores Galore

Shopping for new delights is one of life's greatest pleasures. Table 10.2 will help you find your way to the stores that carry the merchandise you're looking for.

Table 10.2   Stores

The Store	The Merchandise	*Il Negozio*	*La Merce*
shop	everything	*la bottega*	*tutto*
bookstore	books	*la libreria*	*i libri*
clothing store	clothing	*il negozio d'abbigliamento*	*i vestiti*
cosmetics shop	perfumes, cosmetics	*la profumeria*	*i profumi, i cosmetici*
department store	jewelry, toys, furnishings, perfumes, clothing	*il grande magazzino*	*i gioielli, i giochi, i mobili, i profumi, i vestiti*
factory outlet	discounted merchandise	*lo spaccio*	*la merce scontata*
florist	flowers, plants	la fioraio	*i fiori, le piante*
furniture store	furniture	*il negozio d'arredamento*	*i mobili*
jewelry store	jewelry	*la gioielleria*	*i gioielli*
leather store	jackets, purses, luggage	*la pelletteria*	*le giacche, le borse, le valigie*
market	everything	*il mercato*	*tutto*
newspaper stand	newspapers, magazines, postcards	*il giornalaio*	*i giornali, le riviste, le cartoline*
pastry shop	pastries, cakes, cookies	*la pasticceria*	*le paste, le torte, i biscotti*
pharmacy	medicine	*la farmacia*	*le medicine*
shoe store	shoes	*la calzatura*	*le scarpe*
stationery store	paper, postcards, cigarettes	*la cartoleria*	*la carta, le toys, cartoline, i giochi, le sigarette*
tobacco shop	cigarettes, cigars, matches	*la tabaccheria*	*le sigarette, i sigari, i fiammifferi*

If you can't remember the name of the kind of store you want to find, simply ask for *il negozio di* (the store of) and the object you're looking for.

Fast Forward

Refer back to Chapter 2 to look at prepositions and contractions. Use the verb *andare* to say that you are going *al mercato* (to the market) or store. Start with *vado...*

It's in the Jeans

Italy is synonymous with style. Table 10.3 gives you some helpful words to help you build up your wardrobe.

Table 10.3 L'Abbigliamento (Clothing)

Clothing Item	*L'Italiano*
article	*l'articolo*
bathing suit	*il costume di bagno*
belt	*la cintura*
boots	*gli stivali*
bra	*il reggiseno*
coat	*il cappotto*
dress	*l'abito*
jeans	*i jeans*
gloves	*i guanti*
hat	*il cappello*
jacket	*la giacca*

Clothing Item	L'Italiano
lining	*la fodera*
model	*il modello*
overcoat	*il cappotto*
pajamas	*il pigiama*
pants	*i pantaloni*
pullover	*il golf*
raincoat	*l'impermeabile*
robe	*l'accappatoio*
sandals	*i sandali*
scarf	*la sciarpa*
shoes	*le scarpe*
skirt	*la gonna*
slippers	*le pantofole*
sneakers	*le scarpe da tennis*
suit	*il vestito*
sweat suit	*la tuta da ginnastica*
sweater	*la maglia*
pullover T-shirt	*la maglietta*
umbrella	*l'ombrello*
underwear	*gli slip* *le mutandine (f.)* *le mutande (m.)*

The helpful expressions in Table 10.4 will make your shopping even more enjoyable.

Table 10.4   Phrases for Shopping 'Til You Drop

Expression	Espressione
What size do you wear?	*Che taglia porta?*
I wear size...	*Porto la misura...*
What size shoe?	*Che numero di scarpe?*
I wear a size...	*Porto il numero...*
size: small, medium, large	*la taglia: piccola, media, grande*
discount	*lo sconto*
expensive/cheap	*caro/economico*
the price	*il prezzo*
sale	*la svendita*
sales clerk	*il commesso/la commessa*
shoe size	*il numero di scarpe*
shop window	*la vetrina*
This is too...	*Questo è troppo...*
short	*corto*
long	*lungo*
tight	*stretto*
to be in fashion	*essere di moda*
to go shopping*	*fare compere/fare le spese*
to make a deal	*fare un affare*

*la spesa refers to food shopping; le spese refers to shopping, as in "shop 'til you drop."

Smooth as Silk

Silks, cashmeres, wools, cottons, chiffons...rather than spend a fortune on designer clothing, you might consider buying the fabrics and having a *sarto* (tailor) sew something custom-made to your style and fit. Table 10.5 will give you the ability to describe just what you want.

Attenzione!

Colors are adjectives and must agree with the noun they are describing, whether masculine or feminine, singular or plural, such as *i pantaloni rossi* (the red pants).

To describe any color as light, simply add the adjective *chiaro* to the color to form a compound adjective, as in *rosso chiaro* (light red).

To describe any color as dark, add the word *scuro*, as in *rosa scuro* (dark pink). (*Rosa* is masculine unless you are talking about *la rosa*, the flower.)

Table 10.5 Fabrics

Fabric	L'Italiano
acetate	*l'acetato*
cashmere	*il cachemire*
chiffon	*lo chiffon*
cotton	*il cotone*
flannel	*la flanella*
gabardine	*il gabardine*
knit	*la maglia*
lace	*il merletto, il pizzo*
leather	*il cuoio, la pelle*

continues

Table 10.5   Continued

Fabric	*L'Italiano*
linen	*il lino*
rayon	*la viscosa*
silk	*la seta*
suede	*il camoscio*
taffeta	*il taffettà*
velvet	*il velluto*
wool	*la lana*

Something Extra

To convert centimeters into inches, divide by .39.

To convert inches into centimeters, multiply by 2.54.

The regular verb *portare* (to wear/carry) is a good verb to know when trying on clothes.

Dal Calzolaio (at the Shoemaker's)

What were you thinking when you decided to buy new shoes right before your trip? Maybe you want to have your *scarpe* stretched, a heel replaced, or a new shoelace added. Remember to ask, *Avete...?* (Do you have...?), or *Potete...?* (Are you able to...?) using the phrases in Table 10.6:

Table 10.6 If the Shoe Fits

English	*L'Italiano*
shoe	*la scarpa*
boot	*lo stivale*
heel	*il tacco*
shoelace	*laccio da scarpe*
sole	*la suola*
to stretch	*allargare*
to shine	*lucidare*
to repair	*riparare*

In Gioi/elleria (at the Jeweler's)

If you need to go the jeweler to have something fixed or replaced, the words in Table 10.7 will help you get things ticking again. If you've broken a chain and need it repaired, or have lost a stone and want to have it replaced, ask the salesperson, *Può riparare questo?* (Can you fix this?).

Table 10.7 Fix It Again, Tony

English	*L'Italiano*
battery	*la batteria*
chain	*la catena*
clasp	*il gancio*
watch	*l'orologio*
watch band	*il cinturino*

Diamonds Are a Girl's Best Friend

It could be a sapphire ring, a gold watch, or a silver chain that trips your trigger. Whatever your fancy, Italy has a long tradition of fine gold- and silversmiths, and some of the finest jewelry in the world can be found there.

Table 10.8 Jewelry

Jewelry	*I gioielli*
bracelet	*il braccialetto*
chain/necklace	*la catena*
earrings	*gli orecchini*
pendant	*il ciondolo*
ring	*l'anello*
Stones	*Le pietre*
amethyst	*l'ametista*
aquamarine	*l'acquamarina*
cameo	*il cammeo*
diamond	*il diamante*
gold	*l'oro*
jade	*la giada*
mother-of-pearl	*la madreperla*
onyx	*l'onice*
pearls	*le perle*
precious stone	*la pietra preziosa*
ruby	*il rubino*
sapphire	*lo zaffiro*
silver	*l'argento*
topaz	*l topazio*
turquoise	*il turchese*

Mirror Mirror on the Wall...

Women in Italy usually go to the *parrucchiere*, whereas men visit the *barbiere*. While you're at it, you decide to go for the works, maybe even a mud bath.

Some verbs and idiomatic expressions you might find useful appear in Table 10.9.

Build up your grooming vocabulary with the terms in Table 10.10.

Something Extra

The reflexive verb farsi (fare + si) is used when one is having something done to themselves. You already know one reflexive verb: chiamarsi (to call oneself) when you introduce yourself with Mi chiamo... (I call myself...).

Table 10.9 Getting Gorgeous (the Italian Way)

English	L'Italiano
to blow-dry	*asciugare i capelli*
to color	*tingere i capelli*
to curl	*fare i riccioli*
to cut	*tagliare*
to get a haircut	*farsi tagliare i capelli*
to get a manicure	*farsi fare il manicure*
to get a pedicure	*farsi fare il pedicure*
to get a permanent	*farsi la permanente*
to shampoo	*farsi lo shampoo*

continues

Table 10.9   Continued

English	L'Italiano
to shave	farsi la barba
to wax	farsi la ceretta

Table 10.10   Well Groomed

English	L'Italiano
bald	calvo
bangs	la frangia
beard	la barba
brush	la spazzola
comb	il pettine
conditioner	il balsamo
cut	il taglio
face	il viso
facial	la pulizia del viso
gel	il gel
hair	i capelli
hairspray	la lacca
head	la testa
mud	il fango
mustache	i baffi
nail; nail file	l'unghia; la limetta
nail polish	lo smalto per le unghie
razor	il rasoio
shampoo	lo shampoo

In Tintoria (at the Dry Cleaners')

There's a grass stain on your pants from that lovely picnic you had in the *parco* the other day. When you bring your clothing to the laundry, you'll be asked, *Qual è il problema?* (What's the problem?), or *Mi dica* (Tell me). You'll probably have to use the demonstrative pronouns *this* or *these*, so review Chapter 2 if you don't remember them.

Table 10.11   The Dirt on Dirt (and Other Mishaps)

English	L'Italiano
There is...	*C'è...*
...a stain	*...una macchia*
...a missing button	*...una bottone che manca*
...a tear	*...uno strappo*
Can you dry clean this (these) for me?	*Mi potete lavare a secco questo (questi...)?*
Can you mend this for me?	*Mi potete rammendare (these) questo (questi...)?*
Can you iron this ? for me?	*Mi potete stirare questo (these) (questi...)?*
Can you starch this for me?	*Mi potete inamidare questo (these) (questi...)?*
When will it be ready?	*Quando sarà pronto?*
I need it as soon as possible.	*L'ho bisogno il più presto possibile.*

Dall'Ottica (at the Optician's)

You just sat on your glasses and need to have them repaired. Perhaps you want to invest in designer frames. Maybe you want a new look and you have decided to splurge on a beautiful pair of sunglasses.

Table 10.12 The Better to See You With

English	L'Italiano
eyes	gli occhi
glasses	gli occhiali
sunglasses	gli occhiali da sole
frame	la montatura
contact lens	le lenti a contatto
prescription	la ricetta medica
astigmatism	l'astigmatismo
far-sighted	presbite
near-sighted	miope

Dal Negozio di Fotografia (at the Camera Shop)

You bought what you thought was enough film for your camera, but now you need more.

Table 10.13 Say Mozzarella

English	L'Italiano
battery	la batteria
camera	la macchina fotografica
exposure	l'esposizione
film	la pellicola
flash	il "flash"
lens	l'obiettivo
to develop	sviluppare

Nel Negozio Elettronica (at the Electronics Store)

If your computer just won't work, you'll have to bring it in and explain, *Il mio computer non funziona*, and pray you haven't lost any material. A few of the terms in Table 10.14 might also help you get your point across.

Table 10.14 Vocabulary for the Information Superhighway

English	L'Italiano
battery	*la batteria*
computer	*il computer*
disks	*i dischetti*
e-mail	*la posta elettronica*
keyboard	*la tastiera*
laptop computer	*il computer portatile*
mouse	*il mouse*
screen	*lo schermo*

Chapter 11

Bread, Wine, and Chocolate

In This Chapter

➤ Different foods and where to buy them

➤ Expressing quantity

➤ Setting the table

➤ Ordering in a restaurant

➤ Special needs

Food. Italy. The two are inseparable. It's *gastronomia* brought to the level of art. Italians know that fine cuisine is a precursor to living *la dolce vita*. Make sure you eat something before reading this chapter or you won't be able to *concentrare* on anything. *Buon Appetito!*

Something Extra

The word *carnevale* (meaning "carnival" and source of the English word carnal) is no different from the infamous Mardi Gras (in Italian, *Martedì Grasso*—literally, "fat Tuesday"). This was the last night one was permitted to eat meat before beginning the period of Lent. In Italy, two of the most famous *carnevale* celebrations take place in Venice and Viareggio where tens of thousands show up to participate in the festivities and watch the parades.

To Market, to Market

The tomatoes are ripe and the basil is fresh. The words in Table 11.1 should help you on your next shopping expedition. To tell someone you would like to take something, use the regular verb *prendere* (to take), as in *Prendo un chilo di pomodori.* (I'll take a kilo of tomatoes.)

Table 11.1   Dal Negozio

Store	The Product	Negozio	Il Prodotto
bar	coffee, liquors, alcohol	il bar	il caffè, i liquori, gli alcolici
wine bar	wine	l'enoteca	il vino
bakery	bread	il fornaio	il pane
ice cream shop	ice cream	la gelateria	il gelato
dairy store	cheese, milk, eggs	la latteria	il formaggio, il latte, le uova
butcher	meat, chicken	la macelleria	la carne, il pollo
the market	everything	il mercato	tutto

Store	The Product	Negozio	Il Prodotto
fruit and vegetable store	fruit, vegetables, legumes	*il negozio di frutta e verdura*	*la frutta, le verdure, i legumi*
pastry shop	pastry, sweets	*la pasticceria*	*la pasta, i dolci*
fish store	fish	*la pescheria*	*il pesce*
supermarket	everything	*il supermercato*	*tutto*
wine store	wine	*il vinaio*	*il vino*

Fast Forward

Because eating is a favorite pastime of most self-respecting Italians, you're going to need a few verbs to get through any decent meal: *assaggiare* (to taste), *bere* (to drink), *cenare* (to dine), *comprare* (to buy), *cucinare* (to cook), *mangiare* (to eat), *pranzare* (to eat lunch), and *preparare* (to prepare). Don't forget the irregular verb *fare* used in the idiomatic expressions *fare la colazione* (to eat breakfast) and *fare la spesa* (to go food shopping). Try using them the next time you go to a *ristorante* or food shopping.

Dal Negozio di Frutta e Verdura (At the Fruit & Vegetable Store)

Visiting the local *mercato* is a feast for the eyes. Table 11.2 gives you the terms so you know what you're getting.

Table 11.2 Le Verdure

Vegetable	La Verdura	Vegetable	La Verdura
anise	*l'anice*	lettuce	*la lattuga*
artichoke	*il carciofo*	mushrooms	*i funghi*
asparagus	*gli asparagi*	olive	*l'oliva*
beans	*i fagioli*	onion	*la cipolla*
cabbage	*il cavolo*	peas	*i piselli*
carrots	*le carote*	potato	*le patate*
cauliflower	*il cavolfiore*	rice	*il riso*
corn	*il mais*	spinach	*gli spinaci*
eggplant	*la melanzana*	tomatoes	*i pomodori*
garlic	*l'aglio*	vegetables	*la verdura*
green beans	*i fagiolini*	zucchini	*gli zucchini*
legumes	*i legumi*		

In Rome, a favorite summertime treat is *il cocomero* (watermelon), which can be bought at brightly lit *bancarelle* (stands). It's as red as a pepper, so sweet your teeth will hurt, and as wet as a waterfall (get extra napkins). Somehow, the Italians manage to eat the thickly sliced pieces with a plastic spoon (good luck!). Another piece of fruit advice: Italians rarely bite into an apple. They peel it with a knife in one long curl and then slice it into bite-sized chunks, which they then share with everyone at the table.

Table 11.3 provides a list of the Italian for various fruits and nuts.

Table 11.3 La Frutta e La Nocciola

English	L'Italiano	English	L'Italiano
almond	*la mandorla*	apricot	*l'albicocca*
apple	*la mela*	banana	*la banana*

English	*L'Italiano*	English	*L'Italiano*
cherries	*le ciliegie*	orange	*l'arancia*
chestnut	*la castagna*	peach	*la pesca*
date	*il dattero*	pear	*la pera*
figs	*i fichi*	persimmon	*il caco*
fruit	*la frutta*	pineapple	*l'ananas*
grapefruit	*il pompelmo*	pistachio nut	*il pistacchio*
grapes	*l'uva*	pomegranate	*la melagrana*
hazelnut	*la nocciola*	raisin	*l'uva sultanina*
lemon	*il limone*	walnut	*la noce*
melon	*il melone*		

In Macelleria (At the Butcher)

One of the reasons Italian food is so scrumptious is its freshness. Most perishables are bought and cooked immediately. Meats and poultry are best when selected by your local *macellaio* (butcher) who will ask you how you would like it cut. In Italy, if you order a *fettina*, you are given a thinly sliced portion of meat, usually either *di manzo* (beef) or *di vitello* (veal). *Il filetto* is thicker. You find the terms for different types of meat in Table 11.4.

Table 11.4   La Macelleria

Meat and Poultry	*La Carne e Pollame*
beef	*il manzo*
chicken	*il pollo*
cold cuts	*i salumi*
cutlet	*la costoletta*
duck	*l'anatra*
fillet	*il filetto*

continues

Table 11.4 Continued

Meat and Poultry	*La Carne e Pollame*
ham	*il prosciutto*
lamb	*l'agnello*
liver	*il fegato*
meat	*la carne*
meatballs	*le polpette*
pork	*il maiale*
pork chop	*la braciola*
quail	*la quaglia*
rabbit	*il coniglio*
salami	*il salame*
sausage	*la salsiccia*
steak	*la bistecca*
turkey	*il tacchino*
veal	*il vitello*
veal shank	*l'osso buco*

La Latteria (At the Dairy Store)

The only real *parmigiano* comes from Parma, Italy. Most *supermercati* carry a wide selection of cheeses and wines, but you can check your neighborhood stores as well for the products described in Table 11.5.

Table 11.5 La Latteria

Dairy Product	*Il Prodotto*
butter	*il burro*
cheese	*il formaggio*
cream	*la panna*

Dairy Product	*Il Prodotto*
eggs	*le uova*
milk	*il latte*
yogurt	*lo yogurt*

They've Got a Million of 'Em

The Italians have a saying for everything. Some idiomatic expressions related to food and eating are outlined in Table 11.6.

Table 11.6   Expressions to Dine By

L'Espressione	Direct Translation	English Equivalent Expression
Avere una fame da lupo.	To have the hunger of a wolf.	To be as hungry as a wolf.
Bere come una spugna.	To drink like a sponge.	To drink like a fish.
Rimanere sullo stomaco.	To remain in the stomach.	Not to agree with.
Di bocca buona.	A good mouth.	A good eater.

La Pescheria (At the Fish Store)

Ahh, *i frutti di mare*! Go to any seaside village in Italy and you're guaranteed to eat some of the best seafood you've ever had. Table 11.7 gives you a little taste.

Table 11.7   La Pescheria

Fish and Seafood	*I Pesci e Frutti di Mare*
fish	*il pesce*
squid	*i calamari*

continues

Table 11.7 Continued

Fish and Seafood	*I Pesci e Frutti di Mare*
shrimp	*i gamberetti*
tuna	*il tonno*
trout	*la trota*
swordfish	*la pesce spada*
flounder	*la passera*
crab	*il granchio*
halibut	*l'halibut*
herring	*l'aringa*
lobster	*l'aragosta*
mussel	*la cozza*
oyster	*l'ostrica*
salmon	*il salmone*
sardines	*le sardine*
scallops	*le cappe sante*
cod	*il merluzzo*
sole	*la sogliola*
anchovies	*le acciughe*
whities	*i bianchetti*

This Drink's on Me

All that sightseeing can make you thirsty. Table 11.8 gives you the names of some beverages.

Something Extra

As is the Italian way, certain times befit certain beverages. *Il cappuccino* is generally consumed in the morning with a *cornetto* (similar to a croissant). *L'espresso* can be consumed any time of the day but is usually taken after meals (never *cappuccino*). To whet your appetite, you can have an *aperitivo*, and to help you digest, a *digestivo* or *amaro*. As an afternoon pick-me-up, you can indulge in a *spremuta* (freshly squeezed juice).

Table 11.8   I Bibiti

Drinks	*Le Bibite*
beer	*la birra*
coffee	*il caffè*
freshly squeezed juice	*la spremuta*
fruit juice	*il succo di frutta*
hot chocolate	*la cioccolata calda*
iced tea	*il tè freddo*
lemon soda	*la limonata*
milk	*il latte*
mineral water	*l'acqua minerale*
sparkling mineral water	*l'acqua minerale gassata/frizzante*
non-carbonated mineral water	*l'acqua minerale naturale*
orange soda	*l'aranciata*
sparkling wine	*lo spumante*
tea	*il tè*
wine	*il vino*

Fast Forward

If you want a freshly squeezed juice, ask for a *spremuta*. If you want a bottle of juice, ask for *un succo di frutta*.

Table 11.9 lists several *aperitivi* (aperitifs) and *amari* (digestives). Try something new, and bring back a bottle of Cynar (made from artichokes) to share with your friends.

Table 11.9   Gli Alcolici

Gli Aperitivi	Gli Amari
Aperol	Fernet
Campari (bevuto con/senza acqua minerale frizzante)	Jeigermaister (Germania)
Cynar (a base carciofo)	Lucano
Martini (bianco o rosso)	Petrus (Olanda)
Negroni	Averna

Fine Wine

Italian wines are among the best in the world, fulfilling one fifth of the total production. Italian standards for wine are very high, and finer wines are classified as *denominazione di origine controllata (DOC)* or *denominazione di origine controllata e garantita (DOCG)*, which you'll see on the wine label. Other wines are simply classified as *vino da tavola* (table wine), can range in quality, and are served by many restaurants as *il vino della casa* (the house wine). Some wines you might order are mentioned in Table 11.10.

Table 11.10 Bottle o' Wine, Fruit of the Vine

Wine	Il Vino
red wine	*il vino rosso*
rosé wine	*il rosé*
white wine	*il vino bianco*
dry wine	*il vino secco*
sweet wine	*il vino dolce*
sparkling wine	*lo spumante*

Dappertutto (Everywhere)

Do you have a sweet tooth? Table 11.11 lists a number of treats.

Table 11.11 For Your Sweet Tooth

The Candy	La Caramella
candy	*la caramella*
chocolate	*la cioccolata*
cough drop	*una caramella per la tosse*
gum	*la gomma americana*
licorice	*la liquirizia*
mint	*la menta*

A Table Setting

Nowadays, it is considered *maleducato* (rude) to eat with your hands unless you're eating bread. Table 11.12 provides terms for the eating implements and other useful items.

Fast Forward

Prior to the 15th century, most food was eaten with the hands or from the point of a knife. Although it did not come to be commonly used until the 17th century, it appears that *i napoletani* created the four-pronged fork to aid them in eating spaghetti.

Table 11.12   At the Table

At the Table	*Alla Tavola*	At the Table	*Alla Tavola*
bowl	*la scodella*	fork	*la forchetta*
carafe	*la caraffa*	glass	*il bicchiere*
cup	*la tazza*	knife	*il coltello*
dinner plate	*il piatto*	menu	*il menù*
oil	*l'olio*	table	*il tavolo*
napkin	*il tovagliolo*	tablecloth	*la tovaglia*
pepper	*il pepe*	teaspoon	*il cucchiaino*
salt	*il sale*	vinegar	*l'aceto*
spoon	*il cucchiaio*		

It's the Quantity That Counts

Different measurements can lead to confusion. Table 11.13 will help make the metric system much easier to follow. These comparisons are approximate but close enough to get roughly the right amount.

Table 11.13   Measuring

| Solid Measures | | Liquid Measures | |
U.S. System	Metrico	U.S. System	Metrico
1 oz.	28 grammi	1 oz.	30 millilitri
1/4 lb.	125 grammi ("un etto")*	16 oz. (1 pint)	475 millilitri
1/2 lb.	250 grammi	32 oz. (1 quart)	circa un litro
3/4 lb.	375 grammi	1 gallon	3.75 litri
1.1 lbs.	500 grammi		
2.2 lbs.	1 chilogrammo ("un chilo")		

*Prices are often by the etto (a hectogram).

It might be just as easy to indicate a little of this, a little of that, and then say when enough is enough using the expression, *Basta così*. Table 11.14 gives you some helpful ways of expressing quantity.

Table 11.14   Quantities

Amount	*La Quantità*	Amount	*La Quantità*
a bag of	*un saccetto di*	a jar of	*un vasetto di*
a bottle of	*una bottiglia di*	a pack of	*un pacchetto di*
a box of	*una scatola di*	a piece of	*un pezzo di*
a can of	*una lattina*	a slice of	*una fetta di*
a container of	*un barattolo di*	a little of	*un po' diof*
a dozen	*una dozina di*	a quarter pound	*un etto di*
a drop of	*una goccia di*	a lot of	*un sacco di*
a kilo of	*un chilo di*	enough	*basta/sufficiente*
		too much	*troppo*

You Asked for It; You Got It!

You're out on your own, hoping to prepare a wonderful meal. You're planning to start with a light *brodo di tortellini* (tortellini in broth), then you want to roast a *pollo*, and for dessert, some *fragole fresche*, covered with *panna*. Here are some useful expressions you can use to make your meal:

I would like some...	*Vorrei del/della/etc...*
Please give me...	*Per favore mi dia...*
Can you give me...	*Mi può dare...*
I'll take...	*Prendo...*
How much does it come to?	*Quanto viene?*
How much does it weigh?	*Quanto pesa?*

So Many Restaurants

There are restaurants for every palate and every pocket. You don't need to go to a five-star restaurant to eat well in Italy. Some of the smaller, family-run joints have the best food in town. Choose the place that best fits your needs:

Two for Dinner, Please

When you call a restaurant (or after you arrive), you may hear the following:

At what time would you like to eat?	*A che ora vorrebbe* mangiare?*
For how many people?	*Per quante persone?*
Is this table all right?	*Va bene questo tavolo?*
Is everything all right?	*Tutto bene?*

Today's specials are...	*Le specialità del giorno sono...*
Make yourself comfortable.	*Si accomodi.*

*Third-person conditional tense of volere (to want).

The expressions in Table 11.15 will help you ask for what you want.

Table 11.15   Dal Ristorante

Expression	*Espressione*
Waiter	*Cameriere*
I'd like to make a reservation...	*Vorrei fare una prenotazione...*
...for this evening	*...per stasera*
...for tomorrow evening	*...per domani sera*
...for Saturday evening	*...per sabato sera*
...for two people	*...per due persone*
...for 8:00	*...alle otto*
May we sit...	*Possiamo sederci...*
...near the window?	*...vicino alla finestra?*
...on the terrace?	*...sul terrazzo?*
Is there a non-smoking section?	*C'è una zona per non fumatori?*
How long is the wait?	*Quanto tempo si deve aspettare?*
What is the house special?	*Qual è la specialità della casa?*
What is the special for the day?	*Qual è il piatto del giorno?*
What do you recommend?	*Che cosa consiglia?*
I'd like one portion of...	*Vorrei una porzione di...*
The check, please.	*Il conto, per favore.*
We ate very well.	*Abbiamo mangiato* molto bene.*

*Past participle of mangiare.

Table 11.16   Courses

L'Italiano	La Definizione	English	The Definition
l'antipasto	*un assaggio per stimolare l'appetito*	appetizer	a taste to stimulate the appetite
il primo piatto	*la pasta, il risotto, o la zuppa*	first course	pasta, risotto, or soup
il secondo piatto	*la carne, il pollo, o il pesce*	second course	meat, chicken, or fish
il contorno	*le verdure*	side dish	vegetables

What's on the Menu?

Italian food can be found in restaurants all over the world. You are probably already familiar with a lot of *piatti*. Tables 11.17 through 11.19 help you interpret some of what you might find.

Table 11.17   I Primi Piatti

Il Primo Piatto	First Course
brodo	broth
gnocchi al sugo di pomodoro	potato pasta with tomato sauce
lasagna	lasagna
linguine alle vongole	spaghetti in clam sauce
minestrone	vegetable soup
orecchiette ai broccoli e aglio	ear-shaped pasta with broccoli and garlic
pasta e fagioli	pasta with beans
penne alla vodka	tubes of pasta with tomato, vodka, cream, and hot peppers
ravioli di zucca e ricotta	pumpkin ravioli with ricotta cheese
risotto di mare	seafood risotto

Il Primo Piatto	First Course
spaghetti alla bolognese	spaghetti in meat sauce
spaghetti alla carbonara	spaghetti with bacon, egg, and Parmesan
stracciatella	eggdrop soup
tortellini prosciutto e piselli	tortellini with prosciutto and peas
zuppa di verdura Toscana	Tuscan country soup

Table 11.18   I Secondi Piatti

Il Secondo Piatto	Second Course
agnello arrosto al rosmarino	roast lamb spiced with rosemary
anatra con vin santo	duck with holy wine (sherry)
bistecca	steak
calamari alla marinara	squid in tomato sauce
coda di rospo con carciofi	monkfish with artichokes
cotoletta alla milanese	breaded cutlet
involtini di vitello	veal rolls cooked in wine with mushrooms
ossobuco alla Milanese	oxtail or veal shanks with lemon, garlic, and parsley
pollo ai funghi	chicken with mushrooms
pollo al limone	lemon chicken
pollo alla francese	chicken cooked in wine and lemon sauce
pollo alla griglia	grilled chicken
polpette al ragù	meatballs in tomato sauce
salsiccia affumicata	smoked sausage

Table 11.19 I Contorni e Gli Antipasti

Il Contorno/L'Antipasto	Side Dish/Appetizer
calamari fritti	fried calamari
cuori di carciofo marinati	marinated artichoke hearts
fagioli alla veneziana	beans, anchovies, and garlic
finocchi al cartoccio	baked fennel (literally "in a bag")
formaggi vari	various cheeses
funghi trifolati	sautéed mushrooms, garlic, onion, and parsley
insalata di pomodoro e cipolla	tomato and onion salad
insalata verde	green salad
melanzane alla griglia	grilled eggplant
patate bollite	boiled potatoes
prosciutto con melone	prosciutto with melon
spiedini di gamberi alla griglia	skewered grilled shrimp
spinaci saltati	spinach tossed with garlic
zucchini fritti	fried zucchini

That's the Way I Like It

Being able to express how you want something prepared avoids undesirable surprises. Consult Table 11.20 for the proper terminology. If you are looking for a lumberjack breakfast with eggs, pancakes, sausage, orange juice, and coffee, stay home. Italians eat eggs for lunch or dinner as a *secondo piatto*.

Table 11.20 Food Preparation

Preparation	La Preparazione
baked	al forno
boiled	bollito

Preparation	*La Preparazione*
breaded	*impanato*
broiled	*alla fiamma*
fried	*fritto*
grilled	*alla griglia*
marinated	*marinato*
medium	*normale*
poached	*in camicia*
rare	*al sangue*
steamed	*al vapore*
well-done	*ben cotto*
scrambled eggs	*uova strapazzate*
soft-boiled eggs	*uova alla coque*
omelette	*l'omelette*

Spice Up Your Life

If you want it hot, ask for *piccante*, but keep in mind that Italian food is generally flavored with a variety of spices that are subtly blended to create the dishes you love. Table 11.21 describes some of the spices you'll encounter while eating Italian cuisine.

Table 11.21 Spices

Spice	*La Spezia*
basil	*il basilico*
bay leaf	*la foglia di alloro*
caper	*il cappero*
chives	*le cipolline*
dill	*l'aneto*
garlic	*l'aglio*

continues

Table 11.21   Continued

Spice	*La Spezia*
ginger	*il ginger*
honey	*il miele*
mint	*la menta*
mustard	*la senape*
nutmeg	*la noce moscata*
oregano	*l'origano*
paprika	*la paprika*
parsley	*il prezzemolo*
pepper	*il pepe*
rosemary	*il rosamarino*
saffron	*lo zafferano*
salt	*il sale*
sugar	*lo zucchero*

Special People Have Special Needs

You're in great shape and have eliminated certain things from your diet. There's no reason to destroy all your hard work with one visit to Italy. The phrases in Table 11.22 will help you get what you need.

Table 11.22   Special Needs

Phrase	*La Frase*
I am on a diet.	*Sto in dieta. (stare in dieta) Faccio la dieta. (fare la dieta)*
I'm a vegetarian.	*Sono vegetariano/a.*
Do you serve Kosher food?	*Servite del cibo kasher?*
I can't eat anything made with…	*Non posso mangiare niente che contenga…*

Phrase	La Frase
I can't have any...	*Non posso prendere...*
...dairy products	*...latticini*
...alcohol	*...alcol*
...saturated fat	*...grassi saturi*
...shellfish	*...frutti di mare*
I'm looking for a dish...	*Cerco un piatto...*
...high in fiber	*...con molta fibra*
...low in cholesterol	*...con poco colesterolo*
...low in fat	*...con pochi grassi*
...low in sodium	*...poco salato*
...without preservatives*	*...senza conservanti*

*Be sure to use the Italian word *conservanti* and not the false cognate *preservativi*, which means "prophylactics"!*

You Call This Food?

You asked for a rare steak, but you received what looks like a shoe. There's a small nail in your pizza (don't worry, you won't be charged extra), a hair in your spaghetti (yech!), or cheese in the pasta (when you specifically asked for none). Keep your calm and ask the waiter to bring it back to the kitchen using the Italian outlined in Table 11.23.

Table 11.23   Take It Away!

English	L'Italiano
This is...	*Questo è...*
...burned	*...bruciato*
...dirty	*...sporco*
...overcooked	*...troppo cotto*

continues

Table 11.23 Continued

English	*L'Italiano*
...spoiled/not right	...*andato male*
...too cold	...*troppo freddo*
...too rare	...*troppo crudo*
...too salty	...*troppo salato*
...too spicy	...*troppo piccante*
...too sweet	...*troppo dolce*
...unacceptable	...*inaccettabile*

Chapter 12

Is There a Doctor in the House?

You're probably more prone to getting sick while in a foreign country than any other time. You're in a new environment, eating different foods, your daily rituals have been altered, and you're having a great time. Those little bugs know just when to crash a party. Sickness can be especially exasperating in a foreign country where you don't know the names of your medicines and you have to explain to a *dottore* or *farmacista* exactly what the problem is.

What a Bod!

When you were little, you were probably asked silly questions such as "Where's your nose? Where are your ears?" and because you were a brilliant child, you pointed, much to everyone's joy and delight. If a kid can do it, so can you. Irregular plural forms are provided in parentheses in Table 12.1.

Table 12.1   The Sum of Your Parts

The Body	*Il Corpo*
ankle	*la caviglia*
arm	*il braccio (le braccia)*
back	*la schiena*
blood	*il sangue*
body	*il corpo*
bone	*l'osso (le ossa)*
brain	*il cervello*
buttock	*il sedere*
chest	*il petto*
chin	*il mento*
ear	*l'orecchio*
eye	*l'occhio*
face	*il viso*
finger	*il dito (le dita)*
foot	*il piede*
hand	*la mano (le mani)*
head	*la testa*
heart	*il cuore*
knee	*il ginocchio (le ginocchia)*
leg	*la gamba*

The Body	*Il Corpo*
mouth	*la bocca*
nail	*l'unghia*
neck	*il collo*
nose	*il naso*
skin	*la pelle*
shoulder	*la spalla*
stomach	*lo stomaco*
throat	*la gola*
toe	*il dito*
tongue	*la lingua*
tooth	*il dente*
wrist	*il polso*

Express Yourself

The verb *avere* can be used to describe any kind of ache, whether it's in your head or your stomach. You'll also use the reflexive verb *sentirsi* (to feel) to describe your various ailments, as in, *Mi sento male* (I feel badly), in addition to the reflexive verb *farsi*. When using the idiomatic expression *avere mal di*, the final -*e* is dropped from the word *male*. The following expressions will help you describe your discomfort or pain.

I have…	*Ho…*
…a headache	…*mal di testa*
…a stomachache	…*mal di stomaco/pancia*
…sore throat	…*mal di gola*
I feel bad.	*Mi sento male.*
I don't feel well.	*Non mi sento bene.*

(the body part)... hurts me...	*Mi fa male...*
My knee hurts.	*Mi fa male il ginocchio*
My feet hurt.	*Mi fanno male i piedi.*

Something Extra

The reflexive verb *farsi* is used to describe something that is done, as well as what we use to say when something hurts. In this case, the subject of the sentence is the troublesome body part (or parts). If what is hurting you is singular—for example, your head—so is your verb; if your feet hurt you, because they are plural, your verb must also be plural.

*Mi **fa** male la testa.*	My head hurts. (My head is hurting me.)
*Mi **fanno** male i piedi.*	My feet hurt. (My feet are hurting me.)

A doctor or pharmacist will ask you what hurts by changing the indirect object pronoun. The verb stays the same.

***Le** fa male la testa?*	Does your head hurt? (Is your head hurting you?)
***Le** fanno male i piedi?*	Do your feet hurt? (Are your feet hurting you?)

Something Extra

The preposition *da* is used in the present tense to indicate an action that began in the past that is still occurring in the past, much like the word "since."

Da quanto tempo soffre?	(For) How long have you been suffering?
Soffro da due giorni.	I've been suffering for (since) two days.

What Ails You?

There's no need to be shy about what you're experiencing—if you want to get better, that is. Are you constipated? Do you have diarrhea? Got your period? Italians are people too, and they experience the same kinds of ailments you do. The doctor may ask you a few questions, some of which are included here. Naturally, the *Lei* form of the verb is used to maintain a professional relationship.

What is the problem?	*Qual è il problema?*
How do you feel?	*Come si sente?*
How old are you?	*Quanti anni ha?*
(For) How long have you been suffering?	*Da quanto tempo soffre?*
Are you taking any medications?	*Prende delle medicine?*
Do you have any allergies?	*Ha delle allergie?*
Do you suffer from...?	*Soffre di...?*

| Have you had…? | *Ha avuto…?* |
| What hurts you? | *Che cosa Le fa male?* |

Fast Forward

Imagine you are telling a doctor what your aches and pains are. If you are using the expression *Mi fa male…* or *Mi fanno male…*

Example: your head

Phrase: Mi fa male la testa. *or* Ho mal di testa.

This Isn't Funny Anymore

Bad things happen to good people. You may have a serious medical condition that warrants immediate attention. Don't hesitate to contact a doctor or call for help.

Table 12.2 Symptoms and Conditions

Symptom	*Il Sintomo*
abscess	*un ascesso*
blister	*la vescica*
blood	*il sangue*
broken bone	*un osso rotto*
bruise	*un livido*
bump	*una tumefazione*
burn	*una scottatura*
chills	*i brividi*

Symptom	Il Sintomo
constipation	*la stitichezza*
cough	*una tosse*
cramps	*i crampi*
diarrhea	*la diarrea*
rash	*un'irritazione*
sprain	*una distorsione*
stomachache	*il mal di stomaco*
dizziness	*le vertigini*
exhaustion	*l'esaurimento*
fever	*una febbre*
fracture	*una frattura*
headache	*il mal di testa*
indigestion	*l'indigestion*
insomnia	*l'insonnia*
lump (on the head)	*un bernoccolo*
migraine	*un'emicrania*
nausea	*la nausea*
pain	*un dolore*
swelling	*un gonfiore*
toothache	*un mal di denti*
wound	*una ferita*

This Is What You Have

The word *disease* literally means "not at ease." Should you have to visit the doctor, he or she is going to ask you to fill out a form, tell about any medications you're taking, and answer questions about pre-existing medical conditions. Table 12.3 offers you some helpful, if unpleasant, terms to describe health.

Table 12.3   **Conditions and Diseases**

Illness	*La Malattia*	Illness	*La Malattia*
angina	*l'angina*	cancer	*il cancro*
appendicitis	*l'appendicite*	cold	*il raffreddore*
asthma	*l'asma*	diabetes	*il diabete*
bronchitis	*la bronchite*	drug addiction	*la tossicodipendenza*
dysentery	*la dissenteria*	pneumonia	*la polmonite*
flu	*l'influenza*	polio	*la poliomielite*
German measles	*la rosolia*	smallpox	*il vaiolo*
gout	*la gotta*	stroke	*il colpo apoplettico*
heart attack	*l'infarto*	sunstroke	*il colpo di sole*
hemophilia	*l'emofilia*	tetanus	*il tetano*
hepatitis	*l'epatite*	tuberculosis	*la tubercolosi*
measles	*il morbillo*	whooping cough	*la pertosse*
mumps	*gli orecchioni*		

Your doctor may give you a *ricetta medica* (prescription) to be filled at the *farmacia* or *drogheria*.

Alla Farmacia (at the Pharmacy)

A visit to the *farmacia* can solve many of your problems as well as provide prescriptions, vitamins, and assorted sundries. Pick up some *vitamina C* to get your system back in sync, buy some *aspirina* for your head, or smooth some moisturizer all over your body.

Table 12.4   **Drugstore Items**

English	*L'Italiano*
ace bandage	*la fascia elastica*
antibiotics	*gli antibiotici*

English	L'Italiano
antiseptic	*l'antisettico*
aspirin	*l'aspirina*
Band-Aids	*i cerotti*
body lotion	*la lozione*
baby bottle	*il biberon*
castor oil	*l'olio di ricino*
condoms	*i preservativi*
cotton balls	*i batuffoli di ovatta*
cotton swabs (for ears)	*i tamponi per le orecchie*
cough syrup	*lo sciroppo per la tosse*
deodorant	*il deodorante*
depilatory wax	*la ceretta depilatoria*
diapers	*i pannolini*
eye drops	*le gocce per gli occhi*
floss	*il filo interdentale*
gauze bandage	*la fascia*
heating pad	*l'impacco caldo*
ice pack	*la borsa del ghiaccio*
laxative	*il lassativo*
mirror	*lo specchio*
needle and thread	*l'ago e filo*
nose drops	*le gocce per il naso*
pacifier	*il ciuccio*
pills	*le pastiglie*
prescription	*la ricetta medica*
razor	*il rasoio*
safety pin	*la spilla di sicurezza*
sanitary napkins	*gli assorbenti*
scissors	*le forbici*

continues

Table 12.4   Continued

English	L'Italiano
shaving cream	*la crema da barba*
sleeping pill	*il sonnifero*
soap	*il sapone*
syringe	*la siringa*
talcum powder	*il talco*
tampons	*i tamponi*
thermometer	*il termometro*
tissues	*i fazzoletti*
toothbrush	*lo spazzolino da denti*
toothpaste	*il dentifricio*
tweezers	*le pinzette*
vitamins	*le vitamine*

Suppose you can't find what you're looking for or they're out of stock. The following sentences all express possible questions you may have for the pharmacist:

Do I need a prescription?	*Mi serve una ricetta?*
Do you know where I can find...?	*Sa dove posso trovare...?*
Is there another pharmacy nearby?	*C'è un'altra farmacia qui vicino?*
Is there an all-night pharmacy?	*C'è una farmacia notturna?*

Reflexive Verbs

Reflexive verbs are easily identified by the *-si* attached at the end of the infinitive. They are called reflexive because the action of the verb reflects back to the subject and require the additonal use of *reflexive pronouns*. If you want to tell the doctor you don't feel well, you would say, *Mi sento male*. Take a look at the reflexive pronouns:

Something Extra

Reflexive verbs follow the same rules of conjugation as any other *-are*, *-ere*, or *-ire* verb, but can always be identified by the *-si* that follows the infinitive. Some verbs, such as *sentire*, can mean two different things depending on whether or not they are reflexive. As a regular *-ire* verb, it can mean "to hear," as in *Sento la musica* (I hear the music), or "to smell," as in *Sento il profumo* (I smell the perfume). As a reflexive verb, *sentirsi* means "to feel," as in *Mi sento bene* (I feel well).

Table 12.5 Reflexive Pronouns

Singular	Plural
mi (myself)	*ci* (ourselves)
ti (yourself)	*vi* (yourselves)
si (Yourself, himself/herself)	*si* (themselves)

Look how these pronouns work with the verb *sentirsi* (to feel).

Table 12.6 Sentirsi (to feel)

L'Italiano	English
mi sento	I feel
ti senti	you feel

continues

Table 12.6   Continued

L'Italiano	English
si sente	he/she feels; You feel
ci sentiamo	we feel
vi sentite	you feel
si sentono	they feel

Il Passato Prossimo (The Present Perfect)

In order to explain your medical history, you're going to need to know the *passato prossimo*, equal in usage to the simple past tense in English, as in "I forgot," "I ate," and the present perfect, as in "I have forgotten," "I have eaten."

The *passato prossimo* requires the use of the helping (or auxiliary) verbs *avere* and *essere*. You use a compound tense whenever you say that you *have done* something. In Italian, all transitive verbs (verbs that take a direct object) require the use of the auxiliary verb *avere*. All intransitive verbs (verbs taking an indirect object) require the use of *essere*.

Constructing the Past Participle

When you use the *passato prossimo*, you need a past participle. For example, in English you use the helping verb *have* plus the participle (as in, *have* wished/finished/ studied). Most of the time these participles are regular, but English also has several irregular past participles (had/ been/sang). The same goes for Italian.

As you recall from Chapter 3, Italian has three principal verb families (*-are*, *-ere*, and *-ire*). To make the past participle from an infinitive, you hold onto the stem and add the appropriate ending, as shown in Table 12.7.

Table 12.7 Endings for the Past Participle

Endings			Infinitive		Participle
-are	→	-ato	lav/are	→	lavato (washed)
-ere	→	-uto	cred/ere	→	creduto (believed)
-ire	→	-ito	cap/ire	→	capito (understood)

Forming the Past with Avere

The good news is that when used with transitive verbs, the past participle doesn't change. The only thing you need to conjugate is your helping verb and add your participle. Look at the verb *lavare* (to wash) in Table 12.8 to better understand how this works.

Table 12.8 The Present Perfect Using Avere: Lavare

L'Italiano	English
io **ho lavato**	I (have) washed
tu **hai lavato**	you (have) washed
lui/lei/Lei **ha lavato**	he/she (has) washed You (have) washed
noi **abbiamo lavato**	we (have) washed
voi **avete lavato**	you (have) washed
loro **hanno lavato**	they (have) washed

➤ When negating something in the past, the word *non* comes before the helping verb:

   Non ho mangiato molto.   I didn't eat much.

➤ Adverbs related to time are placed between the auxiliary verb and the past participle:

*Hai **già** mangiato?*	Have you **already** eaten?
*Non ho **mai** visto il film Cinema Paradiso.*	I have **never** seen the movie Cinema Paradiso.

Some commonly used irregular past participles with *avere* are shown in Table 12.9

Attenzione!

➤ Transitive verbs (verbs that take a direct object) use *avere* as an auxiliary verb, whereas intransitive verbs use *essere*.

➤ Many *-ere* verbs have irregular past participles.

➤ All reflexive verbs requires *essere* as their auxiliary verb.

➤ One trick to remember which auxiliary verb to use is this: Verbs of locomotion such as *andare* (to go), *venire* (to come), *uscire* (to go out/exit), and *entrare* (to enter) are intransitive and take *essere*. Verbs such as *mangiare* (to eat) and *studiare* (to study) are transitive and take *avere*.

Table 12.9 Commonly Used Irregular Past Participles with Avere

Verb	Past Participle	Meaning
aprire	*aperto*	to open/opened
bere	*bevuto*	to drink/drunk
chiedere	*chiesto*	to ask/asked

Verb	Past Participle	Meaning
chiudere	*chiuso*	to close/closed
conoscere	*conosciuto*	to know (someone)/known
correre	*corso*	to run/ran
decidere	*deciso*	to decide/decided
dire	*detto*	to say/said
leggere	*letto*	to read/read
mettere	*messo*	to put/to place/to wear/wore
offrire	*offerto*	to offer/offered
perdere	*perso*	to lose/lost
prendere	*preso*	to take/took
rispondere	*risposto*	to respond/responded
rompere	*rotto*	to break/broke
scrivere	*scritto*	to write/wrote
spendere	*speso*	to spend/spent
vedere	*visto*	to see/saw
vincere	*vinto*	to win/won

Forming the Past with Essere

Whenever *essere* is used as the auxiliary verb, the participle is still formed by adding the appropriate ending to the stem of the verb. However, *the participle must reflect both gender and plurality* with the subject, as in the phrase, *Gabriella è andata in Italia* (Gabriella went to Italy).

Take a look at how the verb *andare* is used in Table 12.10. Pay particular attention to how the endings change in the plural (*noi, voi, loro*):

Table 12.10 The Present Perfect Using Essere: Andare

L'Italiano	English
io **sono anadato/a**	I went (have gone)
tu **sei andato/a**	you went (have gone)
lui/lei/Lei **è andato/a**	he/she went (has gone)
	You went (have gone)
noi **siamo andati/e**	we went (have gone)
voi **siete andati/e**	you went (have gone)
loro **sono andati/e**	they went (have gone)

Attenzione!

Reflexive verbs always use *essere* as their helping verb, as in *Mi sono svegliato presto* (I woke up early). Don't forget to include your reflexive pronouns before the helping verb and make sure your participle reflects the gender and number of the subject.

Table 12.11 contains a list of the most commonly used intransitive verbs conjugated with *essere*.

Table 12.11 Intransitive Verbs Commonly Used with Essere

Verb	Past Participle	Meaning
andare	andato	to go
arrivare	arrivato	to arrive

Verb	Past Participle	Meaning
dispiacere	*dispiaciuto*	to be sorry
diventare	*diventato*	to become
entrare	*entrato*	to enter
essere	*stato**	to be
ingrassare	*ingrassato*	to gain weight
morire	*morto**	to die
nascere	*nato**	to be born
partire	*partito*	to leave
piacere	*piaciuto**	to be pleasing
rimanere	*rimasto**	to remain
ritornare	*ritornato*	to return
stare	*stato**	to stay
tornare	*tornato*	to return
uscire	*uscito*	to go out
venire	*venuto*	to come

*Irregular participle.

Chapter 13

Conducting Business

In This Chapter

➤ Using the telephone

➤ Visiting the post office

➤ Writing a letter

➤ Banking terms

Whether for business or pleasure, there are a few skills that can take you a long way: making a phone call, writing a letter and being able to read the small print in a business contract or bank statement.

Il Telefono (The Telephone)

Most numbers in Italy start with 0 plus the area code followed by the number. To get an operator, you must dial 15; to get an international operator, dial 170. For an emergency or to get the *la polizia* dial 113, or for *i carabinieri* dial 112. It's always a good idea to find out any local numbers that you might need in a quandary.

Table 13.1   Types of Calls

Type of Call	La Telefonata
collect call	*una telefonata a carico del destinatario*
credit-card call	*una telefonata con carta di credito*
long-distance call	*una telefonata interurbana*
intercontinental call	*una telefonata intercontinentale*
international call (Europe)	*una telefonata internazionale*
person-to-person call	*una telefonata con preavviso*
local call	*una telefonata urbana*

Say What?

Speaking on the telephone in a foreign language can be stressful because you don't have the added benefit of body language to help get your point across. Writing down what you want to say before you make a call will help you ask for whom or what you need. The words and phrases in Table 13.2 should help you get your point across.

Table 13.2   Ice Breakers

English	L'Italiano
With whom do I speak?	*Con chi parlo?*
I would like to make a phone call.	*Vorrei fare una telefonata.*
Do you sell telephone cards?	*Vendete schede telefoniche?*
Hello!*	*Pronto!*
Is...there?	*C'è...?*
It's...(your name)	*Sono...(il tuo nome)*

English	L'Italiano
I'd like to speak with...	*Vorrei parlare con...*
I'll call back later.	*Richiamo più tardi.*

Used only on the telephone and literally meaning "Ready!"

Problemi

You can run into many *problemi* when you're making a phone call. You may dial the wrong number or hear a recording telling you the number is no longer in service. The following are some phrases you might hear or want to say to an operator. They may be in the past tense, so keep an ear out for the auxiliary verbs and their participles.

What you might say:

I have a problem.	*Ho un problema.*
The line was disconnected.	*È caduta la linea.*
The line is always busy.	*La linea è sempre occupata.*
Excuse me, I dialed the wrong number.	*Mi scusi, ho sbagliato numero.*
I can't get a line.	*Non posso prendere la linea.*
May I speak with an international operator?	*Posso parlare con un operatore internazionale?*
Can you connect me with...?	*Mi può mettere in comunicazione con...?*
I don't speak Italian very well.	*Non parlo l'italiano molto bene.*

What the operator might say:

What number did you dial?	*Che numero ha fatto?*
No one is answering.	*Non risponde.*
This (that) number is out of service.	*Questo (quel) numero di telefono è fuori servizio.*
This (that) number does not work.	*Questo (quel) numero non funziona.*
Please hold.	*Siete pregati di attendere.*

Before your fingers do any walking with the Yellow Pages (which is a handy reference for more than just phone numbers—check it out for listings of museum hours, places to go, and things to do), familiarize yourself with the terms related to the telephone in Table 13.3.

Table 13.3   The Telephone

The Telephone	*Il Telefono*
800 number (free)	*il numero verde*
answering machine	*la segreteria telefonica*
area code	*il prefisso*
booth	*la cabina telefonica*
cellular phone	*il telefonino/il cellulare*
coin return	*la restituzione monete*
line	*la linea*
message	*il messaggio*
operator	*l'operatore*
phone card	*la scheda telefonica*
public phone	*il telefono pubblico*

The Telephone	*Il Telefono*
telephone book	*l'elenco telefonico*
telephone call	*la telefonata*
token	*il gettone*
Yellow Pages	*le pagine gialle*

Some useful verbs and expressions related to the telephone might come in handy.

Table 13.4   Phone Phrases and Verbs

The Verb	*Il Verbo*
to call back	*richiamare*
to dial	*comporre il numero*
to drop a line/ to buzz someone	*dare un colpo di telefono (idiomatico)*
to hold	*attendere*
to insert the card	*introdurre la carta*
to leave a message	*lasciare un messaggio*
to make a call	*fare una telefonata*
to receive a call	*ricevere una telefonata*
to ring	*suonare/squillare*
to speak to an operator	*parlare con un operatore*
to telephone	*telefonare*

Just the Fax

You might have some business to attend to while you are away or need directions to your next destination point. The terms in Table 13.5 all relate to sending messages electronically or through the telephone lines.

Table 13.5 Faxing Lingo

English	*L'Italiano*
fax/fax machine	*il facsimile/il fax*
fax number	*il numero di fax*
to send a fax	*inviare un fax/"faxare"*
fax modem	*il fax modem*
Internet	*l'internet*
e-mail	*la posta elettronica*
e-mail address	*l'indirizzo elettronico/internet*

Rain or Shine: The Post Office

A visit to the post office can bring the most sane person to the verge of insanity. All you want is a stamp, but you've got to wait in *la fila* (line) just like everyone else. If you want to send a *pacco*, you wait in one line only to find out you should have been on the other line. What to do? Take a deep breath and remember: You're not just in the post office, you're in the post office in *Italy*. Things could be worse.

Table 13.6 The Post Office

English	*L'Italiano*
addressee	*il recipiente*
cardboard box	*la scatola di cartone*
counter/window	*lo sportello*
envelope	*la busta*
letter	*la lettera*
mail	*la posta*
mailbox	*la cassetta della posta*

English	*L'Italiano*
mail carrier	*il postino*
money transfer	*il vaglia postale, il vaglia telegrafico*
package	*il pacco*
packing paper	*la carta da pacchi*
post office	*l'ufficio postale*
post office box	*la casella postale*
postage	*la tariffa postale*
extra postage	*la soprattassa postale*
postal worker	*l'impiegato postale*
postcard	*la cartolina*
receipt	*la ricevuta*
sender	*il mittente*
stamps	*i francobolli*
telegram	*il telegramma*
to send	*spedire, mandare*

There are many different ways to send something—some costing more, some taking longer than others. If you don't indicate how you want something to be shipped, chances are it will take the longest route. *Vorrei mandare questa lettera…* (I'd like to send this letter…)

Table 13.7 Letter Perfect

English	*L'Italiano*
by air mail	*per posta aerea/per via aerea*
by express mail	*per espresso*
registered mail	*per posta raccomandata*

continues

Table 13.7 Continued

English	L'Italiano
by special delivery	*per corriere speciale*
for the United States	*per gli Stati Uniti*
by C.O.D.	*con pagamento alla consegna*

Dear Gianni

Pick up some beautiful handmade marbleized paper from a *cartoleria*, and indulge in a fine *penna*. You don't have to write a lot; a couple of lines letting someone know you appreciate him or her goes a long way.

Table 13.8 La Lettera

Letter	La Lettera
Dear (informal)	*Caro/a*
Dear (formal)	*Egregio/a*
Affectionately	*Affettuosamente*
Cordially (formal)	*Cordialmente*
Yours (informal)	*Il tuo/la tua*
Sincerely (formal)	*Sinceramente*
A hug (informal)	*Un abbraccio*

Bank on It

Let's face it, banking terms are neither sexy nor fun, but they are absolutely necessary. *Soldi* talks, and so do you.

Something Extra

Founded in 1472, Monte dei Paschi di Siena is one of the oldest banks in the world. The official currency used at the time was the *florin* (named after Florence) but credit as we know it today was an alien concept until the creation of the *cambiale*—the first example of an official document stating one's debt to another. In today's world, we call this a check.

Table 13.9 Mini Dictionary of Banking Terms

The Bank	*La Banca*
automated teller machine	*Bancomat/lo sportello*
balance	*l'estratto conto*
bank	*la banca*
bank account	*il conto bancario*
bill	*la bolletta*
branch	*la filiale*
cash	*contanti*
cashier	*il cassiere*
change	*gli spiccioli*
change (transaction)	*il cambio*
check	*l'assegno*
checkbook	*il libretto degli assegni*
checking account	*il conto corrente*
coins	*le monete*
credit	*il credito*

continues

Table 13.9 Continued

The Bank	*La Banca*
currency (foreign)	*la valuta*
customer	*il cliente*
debt	*il debito*
deposit	*il deposito*
down payment	*l'anticipo*
exchange rate	*il tasso di scambio*
final payment	*il saldo*
guarantee	*la garanzia*
holder	*il titolare*
installment plan	*il piano di pagamento*
interest	*l'interesse*
investment	*l'investimento*
loan	*il prestito*
money	*i soldi/il denaro*
monthly statement	*l'estratto conto*
mortgage	*il mutuo*
payment	*il pagamento*
rate	*la rata*
receipt	*la ricevuta*
sale	*la vendita*
savings account/savings book	*il libretto di risparmio*
signature	*la firma*
stock	*l'azione*
sum	*la somma*
teller	*l'impiegato di banca*
to borrow	*prendere in prestito*
total	*il totale*
traveler's check	*travel check*
window	*lo sportello*

Do you need to cancel a check? Open an account? Take out a loan to continue your fabulous Italian vacation? You may need to know the verbs in Table 13.10.

Table 13.10   Banking Lingo

Verb	Il Verbo
to annul/cancel	*annullare*
to cash	*incassare*
to change money	*cambiare i soldi*
to close an account	*chiudere il conto*
to deposit	*depositare*
to endorse	*girare*
to fill out (a form)	*riempire/compilare*
to go to the bank	*andare in banca*
to invest	*investire*
to loan	*prestare*
to manage	*occuparsi*
to open an account	*aprire un conto*
to pay by check	*pagare con assegno*
to pay cash	*pagare in contanti*
to save	*risparmiare*
to sign	*firmare*
to take out a loan	*prendere in prestito*
to transfer	*trasferire*
to withdraw	*ritirare*

Chapter 14

Home Sweet Home

In This Chapter

➤ Apartments and houses

➤ Rooms, furnishings, and amenities

➤ Idiomatic expressions

➤ The imperfect tense

Some people visit Italy and never leave. If you're one of the many who have fallen in love with the beautiful panoramas, wonderful food, and warm people, you may want to invest in a house or villa (or maybe even a castle!) nestled deeply within the Italian countryside. Should you decide to stay awhile, this chapter will help you make your fantasy come true.

Your Home Away from Home

You're interested in finding out how everyday life is in Italy, and you want to give it a test run before taking the plunge. Pick up a local paper and comb through the real estate section. How many bedrooms does it have? Is there a balcony? Table 14.1 lists the various features people look for in a home. Use the expression *Ce l'ha...* (Does it have...) to ask for what you want.

Table 14.1   Internal Affairs

English	L'Italiano
air conditioning	*l'aria condizionata*
apartment	*l'appartamento*
attic	*la soffitta*
backyard	*il giardino*
balcony	*il balcone*
basement	*la cantina*
bathroom	*il bagno*
bathtub	*la vasca da bagno*
bedroom	*la camera da letto*
building	*il palazzo*
ceiling	*il soffitto*
courtyard	*il cortile*
day room	*il soggiorno*
dining room	*la sala da pranzo*
entrance	*l'ingresso*
elevator	*l'ascensore*
fireplace	*il camino*
floor	*il pavimento*
floor (story)	*il piano*
ground floor	*il pianterreno*

English	L'Italiano
hallway	*il corridoio*
heating	*il riscaldamento*
...electric	*...elettrico*
...gas	*...a gas*
house	*la casa*
kitchen	*la cucina*
laundry room	*la lavanderia*
lease	*il contratto di locazione*
living room	*il soggiorno*
owner	*il padrone di casa*
rent	*l'affitto*
roof	*il tetto*
room	*la stanza, la camera*
shower	*la doccia*
stairs	*le scale*
storage room	*la cantina*
tenant	*l'inquilino, l'affittuario*
terrace	*la terrazza*
villa	*la villa*
window	*la finestra*

Inside Your Home

Is the house furnished, or do you have to provide your own bed? Is there an eat-in kitchen? Curtains for the windows? Table 14.2 gives you the names of the basics you need to live comfortably.

Table 14.2 Furniture and Accessories

Furniture	I Mobili
armchair	*la poltrona*
bed	*il letto*
bookcase	*la libreria*
carpet	*il tappeto*
chair	*la sedia*
dishwasher	*la lavapiatti*
dresser	*la cassettiera*
freezer	*il freezer*
furniture	*i mobili*
lamp	*la lampada*
microwave oven	*il forno a microonde*
mirror	*lo specchio*
oven	*il forno*
refrigerator	*il frigorifero*
sofa	*il divano*
stereo	*lo stereo*
stove	*la macchina del gas*
table	*il tavolo*
television	*la televisione, il televisore*
VCR	*il videoregistratore*
washing machine	*la lavatrice*

Buying or Renting

You'll have lots of questions for a real estate agent or management company. You don't want anyone to waste his (or your) time looking at things that aren't consistent with your vision. Being able to tell them what your *esigenze* (needs) are will help you get exactly what you want.

Something Extra

Current rent laws in Italy make it quite difficult for a landlord to reclaim a property once he has a renter, regardless of the circumstances. Also, if a piece of land has not been used for a long period of time, that land becomes public domain and can be used for a variety of purposes, usually for agricultural or pastoral needs.

Table 14.3 Oh, Give Me a Home...

English	L'Italiano
I am looking for...	*Sto cercando...*
I need...	*Ho bisogno di...*
Where can I find...?	*Dove posso trovare...?*
...the classified ads	*...gli annunci (immobiliari)*
...a real estate agency	*...un'agenzia immobiliare*
I'd like...	*Vorrei...*
...to lease	*...noleggiare*
...to rent	*...affittare*
...to buy	*...comprare*
Is this house available to rent?	*È possibile affittare questa casa?*
Is there rent control?	*C'è l'equo cannone?*
How much is the rent...	*Quanto è l'affitto...*
...per week?	*...alla settimana?*
...per month?	*...al mese?*
Does it include...	*Include...*
...heat?	*...il riscaldamento?*

continues

Table 14.3 Continued

English	*L'Italiano*
…water?	*…l'acqua?*
…electric?	*…la corrente?*
Do I have to leave a deposit?	*Devo lasciare un deposito?*
How many square meters?	*Quanti metri quadrati?*

Some Fun

There's a whole other dimension yet to be experienced in the land of colloquial Italian. A few of the following idiomatic expressions are quite close to English, and many others have similar messages. Did you know that the word proverb derives from Latin (*proverbium*) and literally means "set of words put forth" or "commonly uttered"? Not all idiomatic expressions are proverbs, but often they contain bits of wisdom that can be applied to a variety of situations.

Table 14.4 Idiomatic Expressions and Colloquialisms

Italian Equivalent	Literal Translation	Equivalent English Expression
Chi dorme non piglia pesci.	Those that sleep won't catch fish.	The early bird gets the worm.
Fare alla Romana.	To go Roman.	To go Dutch.
Fare le ore piccole.	To do the wee hours.	To be a night owl.
Dare una mano.	To give a hand.	To give a hand.
Prendere in giro.	To take around.	To tease/joke with.
Andare in giro.	To go around.	To take a spin.
Toccare ferro.	To touch iron.	To knock on wood.
Basta./Basta così.	It's enough.	Enough already!/ That's enough.

Italian Equivalent	Literal Translation	Equivalent English Expression
Che cretino/cretina!	What a cretin.	What a jerk!
Fare una vita da cani.	To live like a dog.	It's a dog's life.
Al settimo cielo.	In seventh heaven.	On cloud nine.
Fuori moda.	Out of fashion.	Out of style.
Essere solo come un cane.	To be alone as a dog.	To be without a soul in the world.
Dimmi con chi vai e ti dirò chi sei.	Tell me with whom you go and I'll tell who you are.	You are the friends that you keep.
Stanco da morire.	So tired as to die.	Dead tired.
Di mamma c'è n'è una sola.	Of mothers, there is only one.	You only have one mom.
Fare il furbo.	To be sly/clever.	To be sneaky.
Fare lo spiritoso.	To be spirited.	To be a wisenheimer.
Fare finta.	To pretend.	To fake it.
Essere nei guai.	To be in trouble.	To be in hot water.
Due gocce d'acqua.	Two drops of water.	Two peas in a pod.
Mancino.	Little hand.	Lefty; southpaw.

When someone wishes you good luck (*buona fortuna*), the mere fact of their wishing implies there's a possibility of bad luck. This might explain why actors and others use the expression, "Break a leg." In Italian, we talk about wolves (*In bocca al lupo*) and the appropriate response is, "*Crepi!*" coming from Latin and meaning, "That he dies!" (Animal lovers may be thinking, "Oh, that poor wolf!")

I Was What I Was: The Imperfect

L'imperfetto (the imperfect) tense describes repeated actions that occurred in the past. Whenever you refer to something that used to be or describe a habitual pattern, you use the imperfect. *Mentre* (while), *quando* (when), *sempre* (always), *spesso* (often), and *di solito* (usually) are all key words you can look for to identify when the imperfect is being used.

The imperfect also expresses actions we were doing when something else happened. For example, "I was studying when the telephone rang." The phone interrupted your studies, which you had been doing for an indefinite amount of time.

Something Extra

Which tense should you use? The present perfect expresses an action that was completed at a specific time in the past; you did it once and now it's over and done with. The imperfect represents an action that continued to occur, that was happening, that used to happen, or that would (meaning used to) happen.

Andavamo al mare ogni estate.	We used to go to the sea every summer.

Formation of the Imperfect

Table 14.5   Imperfect Endings

Singular	Plural
io -**vo**	noi -**vamo**
tu -**vi**	voi -**vate**
lui/lei/Lei -**va**	loro -**vano**

Table 14.6 Imperfect Examples

	Parlare (to Speak)	*Leggere* (to Read)	*Capire* (to Understand)
io	parlavo	leggevo	capivo
tu	parlavi	leggevi	capivi
lui/lei/Lei	parlava	leggeva	capiva
noi	parlavamo	leggevamo	capivamo
voi	parlavate	leggevate	capivate
loro	parlavano	leggevano	capivano

The only verb that completely changes form in the imperfect is the verb essere, shown in Table 14.7

Table 14.7 Essere (to Be)

L'Italiano	English
*io **ero***	I was
*tu **eri***	you were
*lui/lei/Lei **era***	he/she was; You were
*noi **eravamo***	we were
*voi **eravate***	you were
*loro **erano***	they were

Attenzione!

You use the imperfect when you want to say that something happened regularly. The imperfect also describes states of being (mental, emotional, and physical) that occurred in the past and is used to express age, time, and weather.

*Quando **ero** piccola...*	When I was small...
*Quando **avevo** cinque anni...*	When I was five years old...
*Mi **sentivo** bene.*	I felt well.
***Faceva** freddo.*	It was cold.
***Erano** le sei.*	It was 6:00.

Appendix A

Map of Italy

Idiot Speak at a Glance

Table C.1 The Weather and Time

English	Italian	Pronunciation
What's the weather like?	*Che tempo fa?*	kay tem-poh fah
It's beautiful out	*Fa bello*	fah beh-loh
It's ugly out.	*Fa brutto*	fah bRoo-toh
What time is it?	*Che ore sono?*	kay oh-Reh soh-noh
It is...(+ the hour)	*Sono le...(+ l'ora)*	soh-noh leh

Table C.2 Places to Go and How to Get There

English	Italian	Pronunciation
We are going...	*Andiamo...*	ahn-dee-ah-moh
to center/downtown	*in centro*	een chen-tRoh
to the airport	*all'aeroporto*	ah-lay-eh-Roh-poR-toh
to the bank	*in banca*	een bahn-kah
to the police	*alla polizia*	ah-lah poh-lee-zee-yah
to the hospital	*in ospedale*	een oh-speh-dah-leh
to the hotel	*in albergo*	een ahl-beR-goh
by car	*in macchina*	een mah-kee-nah
by bus	*in autobus*	een ow-toh-boos
by plane	*in aereo*	een ay-Reh-oh

Table C.3   Needs, Feelings & Then Some

English	Italian	Pronunciation
Help!	*Aiuto!*	ah-yoo-toh
I feel bad.	*Mi sento male.*	mee sen-toh mah-leh
I have a stomachache.	*Ho mal di stomaco.*	oh mahl dee stoh-mah-koh
I have a headache.	*Ho mal di testa.*	oh mahl dee teh-stah
I am hungry.	*Ho fame.*	oh fah-meh
I am thirsty.	*Ho sete.*	oh seh-teh
Is there a doctor?	*C'è un dottore?*	cheh oon doh-toh-Reh
I need...	*Ho bisogno di...*	oh bee-zoh-nyoh dee
the restaurant	*il ristorante*	eel Ree-stoh-Rahn-teh
the bar	*il bar*	eel baR
first course	*il primo piatto*	eel pRee-moh pee-ah-toh
second course	*il secondo piatto*	eel seh-kohn-doh pee-ah-toh
appetizer	*l'antipasto*	lahn-tee-pah-stoh
side dish	*il contorno*	eel kon-toR-noh
dessert	*il dolce*	eel dohl-cheh
wine	*il vino*	eel vee-noh
mineral water	*l'acqua minerale*	lah-kwah mee-neh-Rah-leh
milk	*il latte*	eel lah-teh

Table C.4   Numbers

English	Italian	Pronunciation
0	*zero*	zeh-Roh
1	*uno*	oo-noh

English	Italian	Pronunciation
2	*due*	doo-weh
3	*tre*	tRay
4	*quattro*	kwah-tRoh
5	*cinque*	cheen-kweh
6	*sei*	say
7	*sette*	seh-teh
8	*otto*	oh-toh
9	*nove*	noh-veh
10	*dieci*	dee-ay-chee
11	*undici*	oon-dee-chee
12	*dodici*	doh-dee-chee
13	*tredici*	tReh-dee-chee
14	*quattordici*	kwah-toR-dee-chee
15	*quindici*	kween-dee-chee
16	*sedici*	say-dee-chee
17	*diciassette*	dee-chah-seh-teh
18	*diciotto*	dee-choh-toh
19	*diciannove*	dee-chah-noh-veh
20	*venti*	ven-tee
21	*ventuno*	ven-too-noh
22	*ventidue*	ven-tee-doo-eh
23	*ventitrè*	ven-tee-tRay
24	*ventiquattro*	ven-tee-kwah-tRoh
25	*venticinque*	ven-tee-cheen-kway
26	*ventisei*	ven-tee-say
27	*ventisette*	ven-tee-seh-teh
28	*ventotto*	ven-toh-toh
29	*ventinove*	ven-tee-noh-veh

continues

Table C.4 Continued

English	Italian	Pronunciation
30	*trenta*	tRen-tah
40	*quaranta*	kwah-Rahn-tah
50	*cinquanta*	cheen-kwahn-tah
60	*sessanta*	say-sahn-tah
70	*settanta*	seh-tahn-tah
80	*ottanta*	oh-tahn-tah
90	*novanta*	noh-vahn-tah
100	*cento*	chen-toh
101	*centouno*	chen-toh-oo-noh
200	*duecento*	doo-ay-chen-toh
300	*trecento*	tReh-chen-toh
400	*quattrocento*	kwah-tRoh-chen-toh
500	*cinquecento*	cheen-kway-chen-toh
1,000	*mille*	mee-leh
1,001	*milleuno*	mee-leh-oo-noh
1,200	*milleduecento*	mee-leh-doo-eh-chen-toh
2,000	*duemila*	doo-eh-mee-lah
3,000	*tremila*	treh-mee-lah
10,000	*diecimila*	dee-ay-chee-mee-lah
20,000	*ventimila*	ven-tee-mee-lah
100,000	*centomila*	chen-toh-mee-lah
200,000	*duecentomila*	doo-eh-chen-toh-mee-lah
1,000,000	*un milione*	oon mee-lyoh-neh
1,000,000,000	*un miliardo*	oon mee-lyahR-doh

Index